D1214934

Poems by

Gerard Manley Hopkins

Poems by
Gerard Manley Hopkins

Selected and edited by
Norman H. MacKenzie

The Folio Society
London 1974

Grateful acknowledgement is made to Oxford University Press for permission to use the text of the Hopkins Fourth Edition and to the Rev. Ronald Moffat, SJ, and the Society of Jesus for permission to use copyright material. Frontispiece portrait specially engraved by Peter Reddick.

PRINTED IN GREAT BRITAIN
by W & J Mackay Limited, Chatham

Contents

Introduction

'Poets of low vitality ensconce themselves like hermit-crabs, generation after generation, in the cast-off shells of their predecessors.' Starting from this delightful quip by Livingston Lowes, an impressive encyclopaedia article could be written on that special species of hermit crab, *Pagurida Victoriana*, the very minor Victorian poet. From the viewpoint of a nineteenth century creative genius, however, who found that many influential people around him belonged to this conventional species, that the reviews and publishers were often controlled by them or their friends, and that his own poetry was considered bizarre because it did not fit into the habit-forming shells in his readers' minds, the subject was no diverting one.

Hopkins had to wrestle all his life against the dispiriting unanimity with which one production after another was criticised. At the peak of his powers he had only a handful of supporters. (Today over six thousand volumes of his poetry may be bought in a single year.) Among the complex of sources behind his life-long 'melancholy' surely lay the lack of warm response to poetry which he knew to be good. Critics earlier this century used to attribute his lack of productivity to an inner conflict between his spiritual devotion as a priest and his innate artistic urgings. No doubt this did restrain him from dabbling when he felt his duty to his students or parishioners called on him more loudly: but then we often wish that some of the more bulky Victorians (seldom memorable in their longest works) had owned less leisure. 'So few people have style, except individual style or manner', Hopkins once remarked in a letter to his friend Robert Bridges, ' – not Tennyson nor Swinburne nor Morris, not to name the scarecrow misbegotten Browning crew. Just think the blank verse these people have exuded, such as *Paracelsus, Aurora Leigh*, Baillie's or Bayley's *Festus*, and so on.'* The sheer voluminousness of the Victorians is disheartening: there is far too much verbal crinoline.

* *The Letters of Gerard Manley Hopkins to Robert Bridges*, ed. C. C. Abbott, Oxford University Press, 2nd revised impression 1955, p. 111.

Like our own century, Hopkins aimed rather at miniaturisation along with maximum performance.

It is true that he had written more fluently as an undergraduate, before his conversion to the Catholic Church; but lines which 'exude' too freely are apt to be derivative, either modelled subconsciously on familiar classics, or sedulously aping the poet's own younger verse. Most of Hopkins's earlier poetry is so unremarkable compared with his most mature achievements that in the selection which follows only the first seven pieces have been taken from this group. The effect which his profound commitment to the Catholic faith had on his work as an artist was to stop him from chattering, from the gossipy verse paragraphs of a professional poet. When the surge comes, a true poet cannot prevent himself from creating real poetry. And the best work by Hopkins was moulded at such pressure that its shape and solidity prevent it from disintegrating on impact with the reader.

An exploration of even such an early poem as 'The Habit of Perfection' (No. 6, dated January 1866), written before his conversion, will reveal the blend of spiritual idealism and sensuous alertness which finds expression in language amazingly resonant. The words seem plain, largely monosyllabic, yielding their sense at a glance. But commonest words have the longest dictionary entries because of their multi-valency, and with Hopkins a dictionary cannot replace the responsive intuitions of a reader. Often his words are unlisted even in the 1972 'Supplement A–G' of the *Oxford English Dictionary*.

> *Shape nothing, lips; be lovely-dumb:*
> *It is the shut, the curfew sent*
> *From there where all surrenders come*
> *Which only makes you eloquent.*

No prose paraphrase can condense into so tight a space the analysable content of such lines. We may pull out the yards of delicate many-coloured wiring in a compact old radio for demonstration purposes, but nothing works until the parts are restored to their original compression. The poem depends upon its sounds and cross-rhythms, the secondary vibrations set up by the primary ones, and also on the capacity of the auditory receivers – ourselves. If the Notes in this edition venture upon paraphrase it is because Hopkins himself resorted to it when his poems puzzled his friends. No pretence whatsoever is made that these glosses enclose all the chords of meaning or overtones of divine truth which may be found in the original phrases. They are merely intended to remove some of the insulating double-glass which may prevent readers from attentive listening. Those who want to probe more fully may turn to the commentaries, to surveys such as the editor's in the easily read *Writers and Critics* series, or the much more thorough two-volume study by the late Professor W. H. Gardner.

Yet a good poem renews itself at every fresh visit. Take the stanza quoted above. 'Shape nothing, lips,' is obviously an alloy of sound and appearance; 'lovely-dumb' not only reinforces this simultaneous appeal to two senses but denotes a serenity of spirit, eliminating any idea that the silence might spring from sullenness, ignorance or vacuity. The allusion to the curfew which follows may surprise us if we do not remember that age-old association between the tongue and fire, dating back as far as the Psalms (39:2, 3) and alluded to by St James: 'What an immense stack of timber can be set ablaze by the tiniest spark! And the tongue is in effect a fire' (3:5, 6, *New English Bible*). Moreover the ancient curfew was the signal not only for the dousing of fires but for silence, the end of the active and social day. It was also connected in popular English belief with the Norman conquest: Hopkins here implies that from the divine conqueror comes not merely the command, but the grace to surrender to it willingly. The word 'shut' finds itself in an unusual context, allied to the poetic phrase 'the shut of day' but abruptly cut off, imaging the sudden closure of the lips. And finally, the claim in the last two lines is no cheap and clever paradox: without the seven years of poetic silence which followed his entry into the Society of Jesus, years during which he wrote only such verses as his superiors asked him for, Hopkins would not have exploded into poetry with half such concentrated originality as is shown in 'The Wreck of the Deutschland'.

A typical Hopkins poem seems to be using a currency of its own. The mere imitator contents himself with the poetic till of defaced coins he has inherited, their milling too worn for the fingers to grip and their legend smoothed by years of battering. But if their content is silver, they can be restamped, given new circulation by a poet who knows their historical worth, their value through association, and their contemporary force in the mouths of gifted speakers. Hopkins came into contact with country workers during holiday tours, and laboured alongside of them as part of his manual activities during his Jesuit training. His *Journals* note picturesque phrases or specialised dialect words which he picked up in Devon or the Isle of Wight, or from the Lancashire ploughmen or millhands he met in the course of his duties.

When he was sent to Ireland in his fortieth year to become Professor of Classics at the Royal University College in Dublin, he gathered vigorous fragments of typical Irish speech for the benefit of Joseph Wright's great *English Dialect Dictionary*. Words like *ballyrag* attracted him; vivid images such as 'He hasn't sense enough to drive a pig down a boreen'; a quaint use of a word like 'boy' ('There's a boy over from the Pope, and Archbishop Croke went on his knees to him'), applied by a Tipperary man to Monsignor Persico, then 65 years old and Commissary Apostolic to Ireland! And another choice sample with a fragment of political intrigue embedded in it: 'If the Pope makes Dr X Archbishop, there'll be *bloody wars*!' Meanwhile in more polite quarters conventional language with its tiresome journalisms eddied around him. Referring to one cliché he exclaimed to a friend, 'how our civilisation is blistered with that phrase now! and the word *grandiose*, which is my daily indigestion.'

The extent to which Hopkins drew upon dialect for word-life and colour is not generally understood: the Notes call attention to some of these virile yokels. The hanging 'honeysuck' is not an affected 'poetic' curtailment, (No. 62, *l*.9), but the older form of the word 'honeysuckle', traceable back to about 725 A.D. and in the Victorian age still applied to the woodbine throughout at least six different counties. The technical terms of all trades appealed to Hopkins as much as their 'gear and tackle and trim'. Yet like Milton he could poise learned polysyllables against homely Anglo-Saxon or Scandinavian ground words.

> *I admire thee, master of the tides,*
>   *Of the Yore-flood, of the year's fall;*
> *The recurb and the recovery of the gulf's sides,*
>   *The girth of it and the wharf of it and the wall;*
>
> (No. 9, st. 32)

Here words which have been used by Englishmen since medieval times (*girth, wharf, yore, flood, tide, fall,* etc.), many of them calling for energetic articulation because of their consonant clusters, outnumber such later arrivals as *admire* and *recovery.* But *recurb* seems to be from Hopkins's own royal mint, set in a context from which its sense surges back to us as from the great seacliffs whose action it describes. The incautious reader should be warned, however, to consult a dictionary when the meaning he is familiar with refuses to illumine the passage it is in. Though the word *realty, e.g.,* is glib in the mouths of North American estate-agents, to thrust it upon 'Duns Scotus's Oxford' (No. 29, *l.*12) is to blunt an allusion to Scotus's contribution to Realism – a philosophical belief in the real or objective existence of universals.

At times Hopkins can be exasperating. He *seems* so intent upon originality as to bewilder commonsense. Even some of his editors have complained about this, but one's respect for his genius increases with one's knowledge of him. Passages which we cannot explicate in logical terms may haunt us with an emotional stir below the level of reason:

> *My cries heave, herds-long; huddle in a main, a chief-*
> *woe, world-sorrow; on an age-old anvil wince and sing –*
> *Then lull, then leave off.* (No. 53)

Here we do not need to query whether cries can 'huddle': the verb somehow feels mysteriously right for grief.

Other passages may respond to more probing. Take his poem 'On the Portrait of Two Beautiful Young People' (No. 59, *st.* 5), where Hopkins addresses a handsome lad, whose eyes look out from the painting, gazing it would seem into the future:

> *But ah, bright forelock, cluster that you are*
> *Of favoured make and mind and health and youth,*
> *Where lies your landmark, seamark, or soul's star?*

The 'forelock' is not merely one of the sitter's attractive features. The cluster of hair is used to symbolise the combination of gifts with which he has been blessed ('make' being, of course, his appearance). Then there is in it also a submerged allusion to fleeting Opportunity, which, as the old Roman proverb had it, wore a fine forelock but was bald behind: once he was let past, he could not be seized. And lastly, young sailors used to touch their forelocks respectfully when addressing an officer: the seagoing metaphor in the third line is thus skilfully anticipated. A scrutiny of the later stanzas uncovers words like 'sway' (*l.*22) 'list' (*l.*25), 'gauge' (*l.*26) and 'furled' (*l.*28), which, whatever their prime function, certainly sustain the nautical underthought. A ship may develop a perilous *list* at sea which was not disclosed by her *gauge* (the depth to which a vessel sinks under a full cargo) before she set out. Hopkins's father, we may mention, was an expert in marine insurance.

Difficulty with Hopkins often arises from an uncertainty about syntax: 'Where is the verb?' or 'Is this a noun?' Thus in 'That Nature is a Heraclitean Fire' (No. 63, *l.*3,) readers whose minds are still full of fluffy clouds from the opening passage tend to misread 'Down roughcast' as 'Downy roughcast', and become rhapsodic over this unique description of a mottled sky. But 'roughcast' (a wall plastered with tiny stones) parallels 'dazzling whitewash'; 'down' is a preposition showing the direction of the darting lights and shadows as the overarching elm tosses with the wind. Such danger-spots are usually signposted in the Notes. We must nevertheless admit that occasionally the experts disagree – a thought which may console those who find his syntax tantalisingly complicated. Hopkins was determined that his poetry was not going to be versified prose, full of grammatical fillers like 'who' and 'which'. What the eye slips over will slide out of the mind. His own poetry sticks.

Nowhere is Hopkins's iconoclastic freshness more evident than in matters of verse form and metre. The sonnet, for instance, had been more or less dead on its seventy iambic feet for half a century or so. But as it is much simpler for the amateur to copy what is misleadingly called 'still life' (*i.e.*, something which is *dead still*), so the interstices of Victorian journals were plugged with genteel sonnets. By the time the second line was reached, you knew pretty well what you were in for. Hall Caine was one of those who determined to publish an anthology entirely composed of sonnets, and Hopkins was invited to submit some samples. But presently came a flurried letter of rejection, written (as Hopkins wyrly remarked) 'as to a she bear robbed of her cubs'. The Object behind Caine's book of sonnets, it transpired, was to 'demonstrate the impossibility of improving upon the acknowledged structure whether as to rhyme-scheme or measure'.*

Later, in Ireland, Hopkins was to find himself thrown up against a fellow Jesuit, Father Matthew Russell, whose collections of 'Sonnets upon the Sonnet', and whose straitjacket rules for wear in that unhappy hunting-ground, burdened the otherwise entertaining *Irish Monthly*. Father Hopkins was allowed to contribute only some translations of Shakespeare into Latin and Greek. Russell insisted upon ten syllables to the line (alternating between light and heavy), and fourteen of these with impeccable rhymes per sonnet, split into the requisite quatrains and tercets. Here are the opening words of some of his specimens:

'My haughty Fair a sonnet bids me make'
'What is the Sonnet? 'Tis a flower whose seed'
'Ye whose aspirings court the Muse of lays'
'Into the bare, scant chamber of my mind'.

How superfluous they seem, wading in their own laboriousness.

Against this let us pit representative parallels from Hopkins, to show the extent of his revolt, or rather the miracle of new sonnet vitality:

'As a dare-gale skylark, scanted in a dull cage'

* *Letters to Bridges*, p. 128.

15

'Summer ends now; now, barbarous in beauty the stooks rise'
'Not, I'll not, carrion comfort, Despair, not feast on thee'
'Cloud-puffball, torn tufts, tossed pillows flaunt forth, then chevy
                                                        on an air-':
– with these openings we feel impelled to read on, from stimulus not
duty. Hopkins experimented with line length, trying six feet (Nos
49, 63), or even eight (No. 47), for various sonnet effects. Elsewhere
he reduced both octave and sestet in strict proportion to create such
refreshing 'curtal sonnets' as 'Pied Beauty' (No. 21) and ['Ash-
boughs'] (No. 58). He extended other sonnets by means of tail-pieces
or codas: 'Tom's Garland' (No. 61) runs to twenty lines and 'That
Nature is a Heraclitean Fire' (No. 63) to twenty-four. Yet both these
preserve the tidal movement characteristic of the sonnet.

The most telling source of new life, however, was metrical – the
introduction of Sprung Rhythm. The simplest form may be illu-
strated from 'Inversnaid' (No. 42), which plays various modulations
on the theme of a Scottish brook. (We might hazard in passing that
the poet seems to be working stanza by stanza *up*stream: having
steamed across Loch Lomond he begins with the brook on its last
rocky stretch, galloping to plunge into the lake, and ends, away from
the tourist crowd, in the weedy wilderness of heather and bracken
through which its earliest course is cut.) Here is its second stanza:

> A windpuff-bónnet of fáwn-fróth
> Turns and twindles over the broth
> Of a póol so pítchblack, féll-frówning,
> It rounds and rounds Despair to drowning.

The stress marks are those provided by the poet. If we take these as
representing the last syllable in each foot and tap out the first line,
it will be seen that each unit is different. Before *wind* we have one
slack (*A*, of minimum weight); *bon* is preceded by the medium syllable *puff*; *fawn* has the hurry of two feathery syllables before it
(*net of*); but the stress then 'springs' over to *froth* without any lighter
material intervening, compacting it into a monosyllabic foot.

The essence of Sprung Rhythm is, firstly, that the length of a line is gauged by stresses, not syllables; and, secondly, that each foot may contain in addition to its stress whatever number of light or medium syllables the artist needs to balance the weight of the stress – varying from as many as five or six down to none at all. Shakespeare had used monosyllabic feet, but his iron-bound editors had assumed that the text *must* be corrupt, and obligingly ruined the effect for him. So in a line Hopkins was fond of quoting Shakespeare's 'Why should this désert bé' (where the stress springs from *this* to *des* without a foot-stool between) the text was either amended to read 'desérted' or 'a desert', or else *Why* was transformed (by Samuel Johnson) into a whining two-syllabled word to bring the next stress forward on to *should*.

Hopkins was led towards the theory of Sprung Rhythm by his study of the rhythms of animated conversation. He could not see why these greater freedoms in speech should not function in verse-movement also. 'The Wreck of the Deutschland' (No. 9) owes some of its fascination to the metrical release that results. In Part the Second the first, second and fourth lines each have three stresses (and are there-fore equally indented); the third and seventh have four each, the fifth and sixth five apiece, while the stanza rolls to a stately close with six stresses in the final line. But what further variety we encounter within this larger variety! A three foot line may possess only four syllables ('Jesu, heart's light,' *st*. 30), or as many as ten ('Of the sodden-with-its-sorrowing heart,' *st*. 27), without straining the elasticity of Sprung Rhythm. But for some of its further complexities recourse should be made to the notes in the Oxford Fourth Edition of the *Poems*, or to my chapter on his rhythm in the Writers and Critics *Hopkins*.

Hopkins frequently reminded his friends that all his poetry was meant to be read aloud. Among the musical effects which he aimed at was 'vowelling off', for an example of which we may turn to another river poem, 'Penmaen Pool' (No. 14, *st*. 6), about the Welsh River Mawddach.

The Mawddach, how she trips! though throttled

If floodtide teeming thrills her full,
And mazy sands all water-wattled
Waylay her at ebb, past Penmaen Pool.

The 'changing of vowel down some scale or strain or keeping'* can be heard in the varied vowels all represented by a uniform 'a' in our historical spelling: how melodiously they alter pitch, particularly in the third and fourth lines. The stanza has to be recited for full relish: *throttled*, a cluster of five consonant sounds to one solitary operative vowel, followed by *floodtide* almost equally dragging, soon sober down the tripping Mawddach. And whatever the silent eye may do, the tongue cannot skip through 'Waylay her at ebb'; the pace automatically slows, reinforcing the sense.

Some people prefer poems like 'Inversnaid', 'Penmaen Pool', 'Moonrise', 'The Woodlark', and 'Epithalamion' because (as someone put it to me) the 'poet there forgets he's wearing a collar'. Yet at least two of the last three remained unfinished, and we may well ask ourselves why. At its outset 'Moonrise' (No. 11) is full of the same sort of excitement which issued in his best Welsh sonnets. Perhaps it was the verse-form which dissatisfied him – this is one of his rare unrhymed poems, and after seven lines he started again in another metre. But I suspect that the sight of one fluke of the crescent moon tangling the mountain, though 'prized' and 'desirable', and sufficient to part him 'leaf and leaf' (taking him out of himself), brought him no further insights or deeper revelation. 'The Woodlark' (No. 12) is also self-enclosed, happy, observant, delicately sprung-rhythmed – but not complete. Again, we should enquire the reason.

In 'Epithalamion' (No. 62), embarked upon as a wedding gift to his brother Everard, the poet was so carried away into his nostalgic fairyland with 'rafts and rafts of flake-leaves light' forming a green canopy of 'silk-beech, scrolled ash, packed sycamore, wild wychelm' above the rock-pools and their 'bellbright' bathers, that the 'gambolling and echoing-of-earth note' drowned the allegory. When, through lack of conviction, he failed in irresolute attempts to equate

* *Journals*, p. 284.

the delightful valley with wedlock and water with spousal love, the poem floundered to a stop.

Completely different are such sonnets as 'The Windhover' and 'Hurrahing in Harvest'. The quality of the observing eye may not perhaps be greatly superior in the second set of poems. Hopkins had, it appears to me, obviously grown up under the tutelage of Ruskin's *Modern Painters*. Compare, *e.g.*, that section ('Of Truth of Earth') in which Ruskin interprets geological forces as the 'internal spirit' within every hill, 'flinging and forcing the mighty mass towards the heaven', with Hopkins (No. 22, *ll*.9, 10): 'the azurous hung hills are his world-wielding shoulder/Majestic –'. Like Ruskin, Hopkins tried always to discover from the behaviour of a particular type of cloud, an ash tree in the breeze as distinct from an elm, a falcon rather than a kingfisher, the precise identifying characteristics of each. Every species of tree had its own way of organising its leaves and branches, to produce a 'typical' outline which countrymen such as Hardy's woodlanders could label at a glance. Such habits of growth produced in turn not only different properties in the timber, but distinct visual personalities. For the sum total of these qualities as expressed in outward shape, yet recognisable only in moments of insight, Hopkins invented the term *inscape*.

'Inscape', however, was not simply an affair of cold scientific classification. It was tied up in his mind with the philosophy of Aristotle, and the teachings of such medieval Christian thinkers as St Thomas Aquinas and Duns Scotus. Unlike the pantheists, who taught that God filled the universe and was equally present in all things, Aquinas saw each created thing or living creature as made by God to demonstrate some fractional part of His own unified and undifferentiated perfection. When therefore one of His creatures (*e.g.*, the windhover) displays its combination of graceful movement with a courageous overcoming of the blustering wind, and with the rich fiery colours of its beautiful plumage, and when this inscape in action is 'caught' by a Christian observer, the response should not be mere satisfaction at having identified the field-marks of a particular species. That is just the birdwatcher's pleasure at ticking off another name in his book. There should above all be a sense of revelation: 'Here is a glimpse of that fragment of His own nature which the Creator instilled into that species'. A sonnet which began with a windhover in full pattern of flight was for Hopkins bound to end with Christ, and with the thought of his own plodding and wheeling along the furrows of duty.*

To regard the so-called 'moral' of a Hopkins poem as a pious after-thought is therefore ludicrously inadequate. Even before he became a priest he regarded the idle enjoyment of natural beauty as an indulgence he should discourage. Under 6 November 1865, before his conversion, we read in his diary: 'On this day by God's grace I resolved to give up all beauty until I had His leave for it'. And during his noviceship he once went for six months in a self-imposed penance, refraining from his usual close observing of the sunsets, the changing cloud arrays above him, and the gradual unfolding of the life hidden by winter as the spring and summer followed.†

'The Wreck of the Deutschland', the longest and by most esti-mates the greatest of his poems, invites particular mention, and pos-sibly also a cautionary preface. Though it recounts with graphic pace the doom-laden course of the ship hurtling in blinding snow towards the churning sands of the Kentish Knock, the poem was not intended as a versified short story. Its middle stanzas celebrate the spiritual vision of a nun whose entire attention was absorbed by Christ the King, while those around were dominated by terror or bereavement.

But more importantly it is an Ode to the divine Master of the seas and of men. At times He may seem to our limited sight a storm God, furious in power, relentless in pursuit, whipping the ice-cold elements into destroying scourges. Yet this is only the dark side of the love which pulses out from the dappled sunset, from the compassionate Christ of Calvary. His apparent cruelty is in fact mercy, as He en-deavours to drive His strayed children from among the dangerous

---

* See Hopkins's *Sermons and Devotional Writings*, pp. 122 ff. The contri-bution of Duns Scotus to his special beliefs is well discussed there, *e.g.*, pp. 338–51.

† *Journals*, pp. 71, 190.

rocks of their self-will towards the 'heaven-haven of the reward'. Part the First opens with an acknowledgement that these seemingly two Gods form a single wise Providence: Part the Second ends with the prayer that Christ may return to England in a triumphant and warmly-welcomed restoration.

Hopkins can be certain of the safety only of those within the Roman Catholic Church, much as he hopes and prays for the wider extension of mercy (see particularly No. 10 and the notes to No. 30). This may raise some barriers against his poetry in the minds of those who are Protestants or agnostics. Coleridge pointed out the need for 'that willing suspension of disbelief for the moment which constitutes poetic faith'. Without necessarily sharing a poet's own creed, either religious or political, by crediting him with the sincerity of his convictions (as we would wish others to respect our own) we can develop an empathy with writers of many centuries and outlooks. If we do not make this effort, whether with Chaucer or Shakespeare or Milton or Pope, we will exclude ourselves from fully enjoying much of our greatest literature, and be largely confined to the contemporary or ephemeral.

With 'The Wreck of the Deutschland' we recommend those to whom Hopkins is new to make their first reading of the poem a selective one. The narrative and descriptive elements are magnificent: the verbal felicity with which he catches in the 'cobbled foam-fleece' (*st.* 16) the innocent soft look of water which may yet strike a clinging survivor like the cobble-stones it also resembles; the metaphysical imagery with which Death parades his instruments in stanza 11 (his 'sour scythe' and 'blear share'); and that wonderful glimpse of a May morning and a star-filled midnight, stanza 26 – a sudden epiphany in the lowering winter gloom. Even Robert Bridges was at first daunted by the ode, but he soon found, as he later told the poet's mother, that the poetry of Hopkins grew on him with every re-reading: he copied the long poem out twice for others to enjoy.

Those who experience the fascination of his poetry will want to study his *Journals*. Open it at his walking-tour in the Swiss Alps (pp. 168–84), or his two vacation visits to the Isle of Man (pp. 221–5,

234–6), or the diary jottings made in the summer of 1866 (pp. 138–147) – almost anywhere in fact – and you will want to read on. Every turn reveals the gift of seeing shifting surfaces or deeper inscapes, and a constant renewal of language, even in such casual weather notes as 'small rain' or 'sky breathing open in blue splits'. And the editors have lavishly added, in appendices, examples of Hopkins's musical settings for poems which sang to him, and an interesting collection of his drawings. Perhaps of even more direct bearing on his poetry is the diary kept during his first stage at Oxford, scattered with speculations about word-origins and word-families (pp. 4–50; see notes pp. 499–527).

The three volumes into which his *Letters* have been gathered provide us with frank and vivid glimpses of his career, from his violent altercation with his headmaster when he was a prefect at Highgate, through undergraduate delights at Oxford, the long years of his training for the Jesuit priesthood, his three years of parish duty, teaching posts in Jesuit high-schools and seminaries, and finally the five and a half unhappy years in Dublin as Professor of Classics at the University College on Stephen's Green. His tone, degree of undress and choice of subject differ according to his intimacy with the recipient, but all the letters show the great generosity of his friendships. Many of them discuss his poetry, his theories of prosody and of style; many more are devoted to keen textual critiques of poems which his friends had sent him for comment.

Finally, no one should make judgements about Hopkins's beliefs without first looking at his *Sermons and Devotional Writings*. It was the misfortune of his earlier critics in the two decades which followed the posthumous publication of his poems (1918) that his religious notebooks were not published: there can be no excuse for the ignorant learned who even today write about him as though they could perfectly deduce his theology from his verse. No profound study of his poetry can fail to benefit from acquaintance with his devotional papers. This volume displays him as a preacher capable of homely language which sometimes perturbed his censors; as a Jesuit who saw in the *Spiritual Exercises of St Ignatius* subtler hints than many of his colleagues did; as a semi-mystical thinker speculating on the fringes of revealed religion; and finally in the utter nakedness of his private meditation notes during the intervals of soul darkness in Ireland.

No hint of regret over his conversion appears, no sense of an ill-chosen vocation. But both in his poetry, his letters and his meditations we find him from time to time echoing some of Shakespeare's laments:

> *When, in disgrace with fortune and men's eyes,*
> *I all alone beweep my outcast state,*
> *And trouble deaf heaven with my bootless cries . . .*
> *Wishing me like to one more rich in hope . . .*
> *Desiring this man's art and that man's scope . . .*

– that either Shakespeare or Hopkins should have felt so isolated and despised (and I see no reason for doubting the autobiographical revelation) is a reflection upon the conventionality of the rest of us. In approaching the genius of Hopkins we have to allow time to expand our limits, to forgive what at first seems his 'oddity' as we too often forgive the commonplace.

Hopkins, a shrewd cartographer of character, knew that we soon become disenchanted with an object or idea acquired without effort. In commending his poetry to members of the Folio Society, I would end by expressing the hope that the Notes provided, while easing the first approach to each poem, will not be allowed to impede that direct relationship between the poet and reader which brings the most fruitful stimulation.

NORMAN H. MACKENZIE
Queen's University at Kingston, Ontario

Outline of Hopkins's life (1844–89)

1844 (28 July) born at Stratford, Essex, near London. His father, Manley Hopkins, a marine insurance assessor, was himself a poet. The family moved to Hampstead, north London, 1852. Gerard showed early promise in art and poetry.

1854–63 Boarder at Highgate Grammar School (which John Keats had attended), near Hampstead. Won Dr Dyne's prize for his poem 'The Escorial', 1860. Became a prefect. Awarded the Governor's Gold Medal and Exhibition to Oxford.

1863–7 (April) At Balliol College, Oxford, reading Latin and Greek. Friends included E. H. Coleridge, Robert Bridges, and Alexander Baillie. Many poems have survived (see Nos 1–7), some in unfinished drafts. For a time contemplated becoming an artist or a professional poet. Some undergraduate essays are printed in his *Journals*. Obtained First Class in Moderations, Dec. 1864, and in Final Schools, Trinity Term 1867. In 1866 he left the Church of England (July), and was received into the Roman Church (21 Oct.).

1867–8 Taught in the Oratory School, near Birmingham, founded by John Newman. Burned his poems ceremoniously to renounce a career as a poet (May 1868). Summer walking tour with Bond among the Swiss Alps, vividly described in his *Journals*.

1868–70 (Sept.) Having entered the Society of Jesus, he spent two years as a novice at Manresa House, south-west of London. The grounds bordered on Richmond Park.

1870–3 (Sept.) Studying Philosophy at St Mary's Hall, Stonyhurst, among the Lancashire fells and close to Yorkshire moors. Summer holiday visits to Scotland and twice to the Isle of Man, described in his *Journals*.

1873–4 (Sept.) Professor of Rhetoric, instructing Jesuit 'Juniors' (some for University of London degrees) at Manresa House. See *Journals* (pp. 267–90) for some of his lecture notes. Summer holiday in Devon.

1874–7 (Sept.) Studying Theology at St Beuno's College, North Wales, overlooking the beautiful Valley of the Elwy. Resumed writing poetry with 'The Wreck of the Deutschland' (begun Dec. 1875), followed by 'The Windhover', 'Pied Beauty', 'God's Grandeur', etc. Ordained priest, Sept. 1877.

1877–8 (Oct.) Teaching and parish duties at Mount St Mary's College near Sheffield. Wrote 'The Loss of the Eurydice'. Then coaching under-graduates at Stonyhurst (April 1878).

1878 (July) A few months as Special Preacher at Farm Street Church, London.

1878–9   Attached to St Aloysius, Oxford, for a year. Wrote 'Binsey Poplars', 'Duns Scotus's Oxford', 'The Candle Indoors', etc.

1879   Three months (Oct. to Dec.) supplying at St Joseph's, Bedford Leigh, near Manchester.

1880–1   (Jan.) Attached to St Xavier's Church, Liverpool. Some of his best sermons were delivered here (see *Sermons and Devotional Writings*). Wrote 'Felix Randal'.

1881   (Aug. to Oct.) Supplying at St Joseph's, Glasgow.

1881–2   Tertianship (or third year of novitiate), at Manresa House. Wrote part of a commentary on the *Spiritual Exercises* of St Ignatius (in *Sermons*). Final vows Aug. 1882.

1882–4   (Sept.) Teaching Jesuit 'philosophers' and undergraduates Latin, Greek and some English, at Stonyhurst College, Lancashire.

1884–9   (Jan.) Appointed Fellow in Classics in the Royal University of Ireland, and Professor at University College, St Stephen's Green, Dublin. Taught Greek and Latin to small classes, but as a university examiner for all the colleges had to mark huge batches of scripts (some with as many as 500 papers) from twelve or more examinations a year. During his five years in Ireland he wrote 'Spelt from Sibyl's Leaves', the so-called Sonnets of Desolation, 'That Nature is a Heraclitean Fire', etc. He visited Connemara, sailed under the Cliffs of Moher, spent short periods with friends at Monasterevan ('On the Portrait of Two Beautiful Young People') and Howth, and in Jesuit Houses at Clongowes Wood and Dromore, County Down ('Harry Ploughman', 'Tom's Garland'). He also paid holiday visits to England (calling on Bridges and Patmore), to Scotland and (most enjoyably) in Wales.

1889   1 May, developed typhoid fever, from which he died 8 June.

1918   First edition of his *Poems*, edited by Robert Bridges. (Appeared Jan. 1919.)

A few suggestions for further reading

Among numerous books and articles the following are easily obtainable:

Brief Surveys and Short Books

Geoffrey Grigson: *Gerard Manley Hopkins* in the British Council Series, Writers and their Work, London, 1955 (paper).

Francis Noel Lees: *Gerard Manley Hopkins* in Columbia Essays on Modern Writers, N.Y. and London, 1966 (paper).

Norman MacKenzie: 'Hopkins' in *The Victorians*, Sphere History of Literature in the English Language, Vol. 6, 1970 (paper);

—also a 128-page outline of his life and writings, with short studies of selected poems, chapters on Sprung Rhythm and Dialect: *Hopkins*, 'Writers and Critics' series, Edinburgh, 1968 (paper).

Peter Milward, S.J.: *A Commentary on the Sonnets of G. M. Hopkins* (Tokyo: Hokuseido Press, 1969). Well worth trying to obtain.

Longer Books

John Pick: *Gerard Manley Hopkins, Priest and Poet* (1942 (2nd edn., Oxford Paperbacks, 1966).

W. A. M. Peters, S.J.: *Gerard Manley Hopkins – a critical essay towards the understanding of his poetry* (O.U.P., 1948. Reissued Oxford: Blackwell, and New York: Johnson Reprint, 1970).

Alan Heuser: *The Shaping Vision of Gerard Manley Hopkins* (London, 1958). Reprinted Archon Books, New York, 1968.

Elisabeth Schneider: *The Dragon in the Gate – Studies in the Poetry of G. M. Hopkins* (University of California Press, 1968).

Paul Mariani: *A Commentary on the Complete Poems of Gerard Manley Hopkins* (Cornell University Press, 1970).

The Fullest Study in English

W. H. Gardner: *Gerard Manley Hopkins – a Study of Poetic Idiosyncrasy in Relation to Poetic Tradition*. 2 vols. (1944, 1949, 2nd edn. O.U.P., 1958).

Note: There are many other good critical books on Hopkins, offering different approaches. The above selection is necessarily a limited one.

Standard Editions of Works by Hopkins

The Poems of Gerard Manley Hopkins, ed. W. H. Gardner and N. H. MacKenzie (London, New York and Toronto: Oxford University Press, 1967; revised, Oxford Paperbacks, 1970).

The Letters of Gerard Manley Hopkins to Robert Bridges, ed. C. C. Abbott (London, New York and Toronto: Oxford University Press, 1935, revised 1955).

The Correspondence of Gerard Manley Hopkins and Richard Watson Dixon, ed. C. C. Abbott (London, New York and Toronto: Oxford University Press, 1935, revised 1955).

Further Letters of Gerard Manley Hopkins, ed. C. C. Abbott (London, New York and Toronto: Oxford University Press, 2nd enlarged edn. 1956).

The Journals and Papers, ed. Humphry House and Graham Storey (London, New York and Toronto: Oxford University Press, 1959).

The Sermons and Devotional Writings, ed. Christopher Devlin, S.J. (London, New York and Toronto: Oxford University Press, 1959).

A note on the text

The text of the poems follows the revised impression of the Fourth Edition (1970), except that where Hopkins provided no title, part of the first line has here been used in quotation marks. Where Robert Bridges invented a title, however, Nos 50, 52 and 58, these have now been enclosed in square brackets to emphasise that they are editorial additions.

Poems by

Gerard Manley Hopkins

A Windy Day in Summer

The vex'd elm-heads are pale with the view
Of a mastering heaven utterly blue;
Swoll'n is the wind that in argent billows
Rolls across the labouring willows;
The chestnut-fans are loosely flirting,
And bared is the aspen's silky skirting;
The sapphire pools are smit with white
And silver-shot with gusty light;
While the breeze by rank and measure
Paves the clouds on the swept azure.

2

Heaven-Haven

A nun takes the veil

I have desired to go
   Where springs not fail,
To fields where flies no sharp and sided hail
   And a few lilies blow.

And I have asked to be
   Where no storms come,
Where the green swell is in the havens dumb,
   And out of the swing of the sea.

'I must hunt down the prize'

I must hunt down the prize
    Where my heart lists.
Must see the eagle's bulk, render'd in mists,
    Hang of a treble size.

    Must see the green seas roll
        Where waters set
Towards those wastes where the ice-blocks tilt and fret,
    Not so far from the pole.

'See how Spring opens'

See how Spring opens with disabling cold,
And hunting winds and the long-lying snow.
Is it a wonder if the buds are slow?
Or where is strength to make the leaf unfold?
Chilling remembrance of my days of old
Afflicts no less, what yet I hope may blow,
That seed which the good sower once did sow,
So loading with obstruction that threshold
Which should ere now have led my feet to the field.
It is the waste done in unreticent youth
Which makes so small the promise of that yield
That I may win with late-learnt skill uncouth
From furrows of the poor and stinting weald.
Therefore how bitter, and learnt how late, the truth!

The Nightingale

'From nine o'clock till morning light
The copse was never more than grey.
The darkness did not close that night
   But day passed into day.
And soon I saw it shewing new
Beyond the hurst with such a hue
As silken garden-poppies do.

'A crimson East, that bids for rain.
So from the dawn was ill begun
The day that brought my lasting pain
   And put away my sun.
But watching while the colour grew
I only feared the wet for you
Bound for the Harbour and your crew.

'I did not mean to sleep, but found
I had slept a little and was chill.
And I could hear the tiniest sound,
   The morning was so still –
The bats' wings lisping as they flew
And water draining through and through
The wood: but not a dove would coo.

'You know you said the nightingale
In all our western shires was rare,
That more he shuns our special dale
   Or never lodges there:
And I had thought so hitherto –
Up till that morning's fall of dew,
And now I wish that it were true.

'For he began at once and shook
My head to hear. He might have strung
A row of ripples in the brook,
    So forcibly he sung,
The mist upon the leaves have strewed,
And danced the balls of dew that stood
In acres all above the wood.

'I thought the air must cut and strain
The windpipe when he sucked his breath
And when he turned it back again
    The music must be death.
With not a thing to make me fear,
A singing bird in morning clear
To me was terrible to hear.

'Yet as he changed his mighty stops
Betweens I heard the water still
All down the stair-way of the copse
    And churning in the mill.
But that sweet sound which I preferred,
Your passing steps, I never heard
For warbling of the warbling bird.'

Thus Frances sighed at home, while Luke
Made headway in the frothy deep.
She listened how the sea-gust shook
    And then lay back to sleep.
While he was washing from on deck
She pillowing low her lily neck
Timed her sad visions with his wreck.

6

The Habit of Perfection

Elected Silence, sing to me
And beat upon my whorlèd ear,
Pipe me to pastures still and be
The music that I care to hear.

Shape nothing, lips; be lovely-dumb:
It is the shut, the curfew sent
From there where all surrenders come
Which only makes you eloquent.

Be shellèd, eyes, with double dark
And find the uncreated light:
This ruck and reel which you remark
Coils, keeps, and teases simple sight.

Palate, the hutch of tasty lust,
Desire not to be rinsed with wine:
The can must be so sweet, the crust
So fresh that come in fasts divine!

Nostrils, your careless breath that spend
Upon the stir and keep of pride,
What relish shall the censers send
Along the sanctuary side!

O feel-of-primrose hands, O feet
That want the yield of plushy sward,
But you shall walk the golden street
And you unhouse and house the Lord.

And, Poverty, be thou the bride
And now the marriage feast begun,
And lily-coloured clothes provide
Your spouse not laboured-at nor spun.

7

Nondum

'Verily Thou art a God that hidest Thyself.' ISAIAH XLV. 15

God, though to Thee our psalm we raise
No answering voice comes from the skies;
To Thee the trembling sinner prays
But no forgiving voice replies;
Our prayer seems lost in desert ways,
Our hymn in the vast silence dies.

We see the glories of the earth
But not the hand that wrought them all:
Night to a myriad worlds gives birth,
Yet like a lighted empty hall
Where stands no host at door or hearth
Vacant creation's lamps appal.

We guess; we clothe Thee, unseen King,
With attributes we deem are meet;
Each in his own imagining
Sets up a shadow in Thy seat;
Yet know not how our gifts to bring,
Where seek Thee with unsandalled feet.

And still th'unbroken silence broods
While ages and while aeons run,
As erst upon chaotic floods
The Spirit hovered ere the sun
Had called the seasons' changeful moods
And life's first germs from death had won.

And still th'abysses infinite
Surround the peak from which we gaze.
Deep calls to deep, and blackest night
Giddies the soul with blinding daze
That dares to cast its searching sight
On being's dread and vacant maze.

And Thou art silent, whilst Thy world
Contends about its many creeds
And hosts confront with flags unfurled
And zeal is flushed and pity bleeds
And truth is heard, with tears impearled,
A moaning voice among the reeds.

My hand upon my lips I lay;
The breast's desponding sob I quell;
I move along life's tomb-decked way
And listen to the passing bell
Summoning men from speechless day
To death's more silent, darker spell.

Oh! till Thou givest that sense beyond,
To shew Thee that Thou art, and near,
Let patience with her chastening wand
Dispel the doubt and dry the tear;
And lead me child-like by the hand
If still in darkness not in fear.

Speak! whisper to my watching heart
One word – as when a mother speaks
Soft, when she sees her infant start,
Till dimpled joy steals o'er its cheeks.
Then, to behold Thee as Thou art,
I'll wait till morn eternal breaks.

8

Jesu Dulcis Memoria

Jesus to cast one thought upon
Makes gladness after He is gone;
But more than honey and honeycomb
Is to come near and take Him home.

Song never was so sweet in ear,
Word never was such news to hear,
Thought half so sweet there is not one
As Jesus God the Father's Son.

Jesu, their hope who go astray,
So kind to those who ask the way,
So good to those who look for Thee,
To those who find what must Thou be?

To speak of that no tongue will do
Nor letters suit to spell it true:
But they can guess who have tasted of
What Jesus is and what is love.

Jesu, a springing well Thou art,
Daylight to head and treat to heart,
And matched with Thee there's nothing glad
That men have wished for or have had.

Wish us good morning when we wake
And light us, Lord, with Thy day-break.
Beat from our brains the thicky night
And fill the world up with delight.

Be our delight, O Jesu, now
As by and by our prize art Thou,
And grant our glorying may be
World without end alone in Thee.

The Wreck of the Deutschland

To the
happy memory of five Franciscan nuns
exiles by the Falck Laws
drowned between midnight and morning of
Dec. 7th, 1875

PART THE FIRST

1

Thou mastering me
God! giver of breath and bread;
World's strand, sway of the sea;
Lord of living and dead;
Thou hast bound bones and veins in me, fastened me flesh,
And after it almost unmade, what with dread,
Thy doing: and dost thou touch me afresh?
Over again I feel thy finger and find thee.

2

I did say yes
O at lightning and lashed rod;
Thou heardst me truer than tongue confess
Thy terror, O Christ, O God;
Thou knowest the walls, altar and hour and night:
The swoon of a heart that the sweep and the hurl of thee trod
Hard down with a horror of height:
And the midriff astrain with leaning of, laced with fire of stress.

3

The frown of his face
Before me, the hurtle of hell
Behind, where, where was a, where was a place?
I whirled out wings that spell
And fled with a fling of the heart to the heart of the Host.
My heart, but you were dovewinged, I can tell,
Carrier-witted, I am bold to boast,
To flash from the flame to the flame then, tower from the grace to
the grace.

4

I am soft sift
In an hourglass – at the wall
Fast, but mined with a motion, a drift,
And it crowds and it combs to the fall;
I steady as a water in a well, to a poise, to a pane,
But roped with, always, all the way down from the tall
Fells or flanks of the voel, a vein
Of the gospel proffer, a pressure, a principle, Christ's gift.

5

I kiss my hand
To the stars, lovely-asunder
Starlight, wafting him out of it; and
Glow, glory in thunder;
Kiss my hand to the dappled-with-damson west:
Since, tho' he is under the world's splendour and wonder,
His mystery must be instressed, stressed;
For I greet him the days I meet him, and bless when I understand.

6

Not out of his bliss
Springs the stress felt
Nor first from heaven (and few know this)
Swings the stroke dealt –
Stroke and a stress that stars and storms deliver,
That guilt is hushed by, hearts are flushed by and melt –
But it rides time like riding a river
(And here the faithful waver, the faithless fable and miss).

7

It dates from day
Of his going in Galilee;
Warm-laid grave of a womb-life grey;
Manger, maiden's knee;
The dense and the driven Passion, and frightful sweat:
Thence the discharge of it, there its swelling to be,
Though felt before, though in high flood yet –
What none would have known of it, only the heart, being hard at
                                            bay,

8

Is out with it! Oh,
We lash with the best or worst
Word last! How a lush-kept plush-capped sloe
Will, mouthed to flesh-burst,
Gush! – flush the man, the being with it, sour or sweet,
Brim, in a flash, full! – Hither then, last or first,
To hero of Cavalry, Christ,'s feet –
Never ask if meaning it, wanting it, warned of it – men go.

9

Be adored among men,
God, three-numberèd form;
Wring thy rebel, dogged in den,
Man's malice, with wrecking and storm.
Beyond saying sweet, past telling of tongue,
Thou art lightning and love, I found it, a winter and warm;
Father and fondler of heart thou hast wrung:
Hast thy dark descending and most art merciful then.

10

With an anvil-ding
And with fire in him forge thy will
Or rather, rather then, stealing as Spring
Through him, melt him but master him still:
Whether at once, as once at a crash Paul,
Or as Austin, a lingering-out swéet skíll,
Make mercy in all of us, out of us all
Mastery, but be adored, but be adored King.

PART THE SECOND

11

'Some find me a sword; some
The flange and the rail; flame,
Fang, or flood' goes Death on drum,
And storms bugle his fame.
But wé dream we are rooted in earth – Dust!
Flesh falls within sight of us, we, though our flower the same,
Wave with the meadow, forget that there must
The sour scythe cringe, and the blear share come.

~ On Saturday sailed from Bremen,
 American-outward-bound,
Take settler and seamen, tell men with women,
 Two hundred souls in the round –
O Father, not under thy feathers nor ever as guessing
The goal was a shoal, of a fourth the doom to be drowned;
 Yet did the dark side of the bay of thy blessing
Not vault them, the million of rounds of thy mercy not reeve even
          them in?

Into the snows she sweeps,
 Hurling the haven behind,
The Deutschland, on Sunday; and so the sky keeps,
 For the infinite air is unkind,
And the sea flint-flake, black-backed in the regular blow,
Sitting Eastnortheast, in cursed quarter, the wind;
 Wiry and white-fiery and whirlwind-swivellèd snow
Spins to the widow-making unchilding unfathering deeps.

She drove in the dark to leeward,
 She struck – not a reef or a rock
But the combs of a smother of sand; night drew her
 Dead to the Kentish Knock;
And she beat the bank down with her bows and the ride of
          her keel;
The breakers rolled on her beam with ruinous shock;
 And canvas and compass, the whorl and the wheel
Idle for ever to waft her or wind her with, these she endured.

15

Hope had grown grey hairs,
Hope had mourning on,
Trenched with tears, carved with cares,
Hope was twelve hours gone;
And frightful a nightfall folded rueful a day
Nor rescue, only rocket and lightship, shone,
And lives at last were washing away:
To the shrouds they took, – they shook in the hurling and horrible
airs.

16

One stirred from the rigging to save
The wild woman-kind below,
With a rope's end round the man, handy and brave –
He was pitched to his death at a blow,
For all his dreadnought breast and braids of thew:
They could tell him for hours, dandled the to and fro
Through the cobbled foam-fleece. What could he do
With the burl of the fountains of air, buck and the flood of the
wave?

17

They fought with God's cold –
And they could not and fell to the deck
(Crushed them) or water (and drowned them) or rolled
With the sea-romp over the wreck.
Night roared, with the heart-break hearing a heart-broke
rabble,
The woman's wailing, the crying of child without check –
Till a lioness arose breasting the babble,
A prophetess towered in the tumult, a virginal tongue told.

18

Ah, touched in your bower of bone,
Are you! turned for an exquisite smart,
Have you! make words break from me here all alone,
Do you! – mother of being in me, heart.
O unteachably after evil, but uttering truth,
Why, tears! is it? tears; such a melting, a madrigal start!
Never-eldering revel and river of youth,
What can it be, this glee? the good you have there of your own?

19

Sister, a sister calling
A master, her master and mine! –
And the inboard seas run swirling and hawling;
The rash smart sloggering brine
Blinds her; but she that weather sees one thing, one;
Has one fetch in her: she rears herself to divine
Ears, and the call of the tall nun
To the men in the tops and the tackle rode over the storm's
                                                    brawling.

20

She was first of a five and came
Of a coifèd sisterhood.
(O Deutschland, double a desperate name!
O world wide of its good!
But Gertrude, lily, and Luther, are two of a town,
Christ's lily and beast of the waste wood:
From life's dawn it is drawn down,
Abel is Cain's brother and breasts they have sucked the same.)

21

Loathed for a love men knew in them,
Banned by the land of their birth,
Rhine refused them, Thames would ruin them;
Surf, snow, river and earth
Gnashed: but thou art above, thou Orion of light;
Thy unchancelling poising palms were weighing the worth,
Thou martyr-master: in thy sight
Storm flakes were scroll-leaved flowers, lily showers – sweet heaven
was astrew in them.

22

Five! the finding and sake
And cipher of suffering Christ.
Mark, the mark is of man's make
And the word of it Sacrificed.
But he scores it in scarlet himself on his own bespoken,
Before-time-taken, dearest prizèd and priced –
Stigma, signal, cinquefoil token
For lettering of the lamb's fleece, ruddying of the rose-flake.

23

Joy fall to thee, father Francis,
Drawn to the Life that died;
With the gnarls of the nails in thee, niche of the lance, his
Lovescape crucified
And seal of his seraph-arrival! and these thy daughters
And five-livèd and leavèd favour and pride,
Are sisterly sealed in wild waters,
To bathe in his fall-gold mercies, to breathe in his all-fire glances.

24

Away in the loveable west,
  On a pastoral forehead of Wales,
I was under a roof here, I was at rest,
  And they the prey of the gales;
She to the black-about air, to the breaker, the thickly
Falling flakes, to the throng that catches and quails
  Was calling 'O Christ, Christ, come quickly':
The cross to her she calls Christ to her, christens her wild-worst
                                  Best.

25

The majesty! what did she mean?
  Breathe, arch and original Breath.
Is it love in her of the being as her lover had been?
  Breathe, body of lovely Death.
They were else-minded then, altogether, the men
Woke thee with a *We are perishing* in the weather of
                               Gennesareth.
  Or is it that she cried for the crown then,
The keener to come at the comfort for feeling the combating keen?

26

For how to the heart's cheering
  The down-dugged ground-hugged grey
Hovers off, the jay-blue heavens appearing
  Of pied and peeled May!
Blue-beating and hoary-glow height; or night, still higher,
With belled fire and the moth-soft Milky Way,
  What by your measure is the heaven of desire,
The treasure never eyesight got, nor was ever guessed what for the
                                hearing?

No, but it was not these.
The jading and jar of the cart,
Time's tasking, it is fathers that asking for ease
Of the sodden-with-its-sorrowing heart,
Not danger, electrical horror; then further it finds
The appealing of the Passion is tenderer in prayer apart:
Other, I gather, in measure her mind's
Burden, in wind's burly and beat of endragonèd seas.

But how shall I . . . make me room there:
Reach me a . . . Fancy, come faster –
Strike you the sight of it? look at it loom there,
Thing that she . . . There then! the Master,
Ipse, the only one, Christ, King, Head:
He was to cure the extremity where he had cast her;
Do, deal, lord it with living and dead;
Let him ride, her pride, in his triumph, despatch and have done
with his doom there.

Ah! there was a heart right!
There was single eye!
Read the unshapeable shock night
And knew the who and the why;
Wording it how but by him that present and past,
Heaven and earth are word of, worded by? –
The Simon Peter of a soul! to the blast
Tarpeïan-fast, but a blown beacon of light.

30

Jesu, heart's light,
Jesu, maid's son,
What was the feast followed the night
Thou hadst glory of this nun? –
Feast of the one woman without stain.
For so conceivèd, so to conceive thee is done;
But here was heart-throe, birth of a brain,
Word, that heard and kept thee and uttered thee outright.

31

Well, she has thee for the pain, for the
Patience; but pity of the rest of them!
Heart, go and bleed at a bitterer vein for the
Comfortless unconfessed of them –
No not uncomforted: lovely-felicitous Providence
Finger of a tender of, O of a feathery delicacy, the breast of the
Maiden could obey so, be a bell to, ring of it, and
Startle the poor sheep back! is the shipwrack then a harvest, does
tempest carry the grain for thee?

32

I admire thee, master of the tides,
Of the Yore-flood, of the year's fall;
The recurb and the recovery of the gulf's sides,
The girth of it and the wharf of it and the wall;
Stanching, quenching ocean of a motionable mind;
Ground of being, and granite of it: past all
Grasp God, throned behind
Death with a sovereignty that heeds but hides, bodes but abides;

33

With a mercy that outrides
The all of water, an ark
For the listener; for the lingerer with a love glides
Lower than death and the dark;
A vein for the visiting of the past-prayer, pent in prison,
The-last-breath penitent spirits – the uttermost mark
Our passion-plungèd giant risen,
The Christ of the Father compassionate, fetched in the storm of
his strides.

34

Now burn, new born to the world,
Double-naturèd name,
The heaven-flung, heart-fleshed, maiden-furled
Miracle-in-Mary-of-flame,
Mid-numberèd he in three of the thunder-throne!
Not a dooms-day dazzle in his coming nor dark as he came;
Kind, but royally reclaiming his own;
A released shower, let flash to the shire, not a lightning of fire
hard-hurled.

35

Dame, at our door
Drowned, and among our shoals,
Remember us in the roads, the heaven-haven of the
reward:
Our King back, Oh, upon English souls!
Let him easter in us, be a dayspring to the dimness of us, be a
crimson-cresseted east,
More brightening her, rare-dear Britain, as his reign rolls,
Pride, rose, prince, hero of us, high-priest,
Our hearts' charity's hearth's fire, our thoughts' chivalry's throng's
Lord.

10

'To him who ever thought with love'

To him who ever thought with love of me
Or ever did for my sake some good deed
I will appear, looking such charity
And kind compassion, at his life's last need
That he will out of hand and heartily
Repent he sinned and all his sins be freed.

Moonrise

I awoke in the Midsummer not-to-call night, ' in the white and the
walk of the morning:
The moon, dwindled and thinned to the fringe ' of a fingernail
held to the candle,
Or paring of paradisaïcal fruit, ' lovely in waning but lustreless,
Stepped from the stool, drew back from the barrow, ' of dark
Maenefa the mountain;
A cusp still clasped him, a fluke yet fanged him, ' entangled him,
not quit utterly.
This was the prized, the desirable sight, ' unsought, presented so
easily,
Parted me leaf and leaf, divided me, ' eyelid and eyelid of slumber.

The Woodlark

Teevo cheevo cheevio chee:
O where, what can thát be?
Weedio-weedio: there again!
So tiny a trickle of sóng-strain;
And all round not to be found
For brier, bough, furrow, or gréen ground
Before or behind or far or at hand
Either left either right
Anywhere in the súnlight.

Well, after all! Ah but hark –   10
'I am the little wóodlark.
The skylark is my cousin and he
Is known to men more than me.
Round a ring, around a ring
And while I sail (must listen) I sing.

To-day the sky is two and two
With white strokes and strains of the blue.
The blue wheat-acre is underneath
And the corn is corded and shoulders its sheaf,
The ear in milk, lush the sash,   20
And crush-silk poppies aflash,
The blood-gush blade-gash
Flame-rash rudred
Bud shelling or broad-shed
Tatter-tangled and dingle-a-danglèd
Dandy-hung dainty head.

And down . . . the furrow dry
Sunspurge and oxeye
And lace-leaved lovely
Foam-tuft fumitory.   30

I ám so véry, O só very glád
That I dó thínk there is not to be had
[Anywhere any more joy to be in.
Cheevio:] when the cry within
Says Go on then I go on
Till the longing is less and the good gone,
But down drop, if it says Stop,
To the all-a-leaf of the tréetop.
And after that off the bough
[Hover-float to the hedge brow].   40

Through the velvety wind V-winged
[Where shake shadow is sun's-eye-ringed]
To the nest's nook I balance and buoy
With a sweet joy of a sweet joy,
Sweet, of a sweet, of a sweet joy
Of a sweet – a sweet – sweet – joy.'

13

The Silver Jubilee:

To James First Bishop of Shrewsbury on the
25th Year of his Episcopate July 28, 1876

Though no high-hung bells or din
Of braggart bugles cry it in –
   What is sound? Nature's round
Makes the Silver Jubilee.

Five and twenty years have run
Since sacred fountains to the sun
   Sprang, that but now were shut,
Showering Silver Jubilee.

Feasts, when we shall fall asleep,
Shrewsbury may see others keep;
   None but you this her true,
This her Silver Jubilee.

Not today we need lament
Your wealth of life is some way spent:
   Toil has shed round your head
Silver but for Jubilee.

Then for her whose velvet vales
Should have pealed with welcome, Wales,
   Let the chime of a rhyme
Utter Silver Jubilee.

14

Penmaen Pool

For the Visitors' Book at the Inn

Who long for rest, who look for pleasure
Away from counter, court, or school
O where live well your lease of leisure
But here at, here at Penmaen Pool?

You'll dare the Alp? you'll dart the skiff?
Each sport has here its tackle and tool:
Come, plant the staff by Cadair cliff;
Come, swing the sculls on Penmaen Pool.

What's yonder? Grizzled Dyphwys dim:
The triple-hummocked Giant's Stool,
Hoar messmate, hobs and nobs with him
To halve the bowl of Penmaen Pool.

And all the landscape under survey,
At tranquil turns, by nature's rule,
Rides repeated topsyturvy
In frank, in fairy Penmaen Pool.

And Charles's Wain, the wondrous seven,
And sheep-flock clouds like worlds of wool,
For all they shine so, high in heaven,
Shew brighter shaken in Penmaen Pool.

The Mawddach, how she trips! though throttled
If floodtide teeming thrills her full,
And mazy sands all water-wattled
Waylay her at ebb, past Penmaen Pool.

But what's to see in stormy weather,
When grey showers gather and gusts are cool? –
Why, raindrop-roundels looped together
That lace the face of Penmaen Pool.

Then even in weariest wintry hour
Of New Year's month or surly Yule
Furred snows, charged tuft above tuft, tower
From darksome darksome Penmaen Pool.

And ever, if bound here hardest home,
You've parlour-pastime left and (who'll
Not honour it?) ale like goldy foam
That frocks an oar in Penmaen Pool.

Then come who pine for peace or pleasure
Away from counter, court, or school,
Spend here your measure of time and treasure
And taste the treats of Penmaen Pool.

God's Grandeur

The world is charged with the grandeur of God.
  It will flame out, like shining from shook foil;
  It gathers to a greatness, like the ooze of oil
Crushed. Why do men then now not reck his rod?
Generations have trod, have trod, have trod;
  And all is seared with trade; bleared, smeared with toil;
  And wears man's smudge and shares man's smell: the soil
Is bare now, nor can foot feel, being shod.

And for all this, nature is never spent;
  There lives the dearest freshness deep down things;
And though the last lights off the black West went
  Oh, morning, at the brown brink eastward, springs –
Because the Holy Ghost over the bent
  World broods with warm breast and with ah! bright wings.

The Starlight Night

Look at the stars! look, look up at the skies!
  O look at all the fire-folk sitting in the air!
  The bright boroughs, the circle-citadels there!
Down in dim woods the diamond delves! the elves'-eyes!
The grey lawns cold where gold, where quickgold lies!
  Wind-beat whitebeam! airy abeles set on a flare!
  Flake-doves sent floating forth at a farmyard scare! –
Ah well! it is all a purchase, all is a prize.

Buy then! bid then! – What? – Prayer, patience, alms, vows.
Look, look: a May-mess, like on orchard boughs!
  Look! March-bloom, like on mealed-with-yellow sallows!
These are indeed the barn; withindoors house
The shocks. This piece-bright paling shuts the spouse
  Christ home, Christ and his mother and all his hallows.

17

Spring

Nothing is so beautiful as Spring –
  When weeds, in wheels, shoot long and lovely and lush;
  Thrush's eggs look little low heavens, and thrush
Through the echoing timber does so rinse and wring
The ear, it strikes like lightnings to hear him sing;
  The glassy peartree leaves and blooms, they brush
  The descending blue; that blue is all in a rush
With richness; the racing lambs too have fair their fling.

What is all this juice and all this joy?
  A strain of the earth's sweet being in the beginning
In Eden garden. – Have, get, before it cloy,

  Before it cloud, Christ, lord, and sour with sinning,
Innocent mind and Mayday in girl and boy,
  Most, O maid's child, thy choice and worthy the winning.

In the Valley of the Elwy

I remember a house where all were good
  To me, God knows, deserving no such thing:
  Comforting smell breathed at very entering,
Fetched fresh, as I suppose, off some sweet wood.
That cordial air made those kind people a hood
  All over, as a bevy of eggs the mothering wing
  Will, or mild nights the new morsels of Spring:
Why, it seemed of course; seemed of right it should.

Lovely the woods, waters, meadows, combes, vales,
All the air things wear that build this world of Wales;
  Only the inmate does not correspond:

God, lover of souls, swaying considerate scales,
Complete thy creature dear O where it fails,
  Being mighty a master, being a father and fond.

The Sea and the Skylark

On ear and ear two noises too old to end
  Trench – right, the tide that ramps against the shore;
  With a flood or a fall, low lull-off or all roar,
Frequenting there while moon shall wear and wend.

Left hand, off land, I hear the lark ascend,
  His rash-fresh re-winded new-skeinèd score
  In crisps of curl off wild winch whirl, and pour
And pelt music, till none's to spill nor spend.

How these two shame this shallow and frail town!
  How ring right out our sordid turbid time,
Being pure! We, life's pride and cared-for crown,

  Have lost that cheer and charm of earth's past prime:
Our make and making break, are breaking, down
  To man's last dust, drain fast towards man's first slime.

The Windhover:

To Christ our Lord

I caught this morning morning's minion, king-
   dom of daylight's dauphin, dapple-dawn-drawn Falcon, in his
                                              riding
   Of the rolling level underneath him steady air, and striding
High there, how he rung upon the rein of a wimpling wing
In his ecstasy! then off, off forth on swing,
   As a skate's heel sweeps smooth on a bow-bend: the hurl and
                                             gliding
   Rebuffed the big wind. My heart in hiding
Stirred for a bird, – the achieve of, the mastery of the thing!

Brute beauty and valour and act, oh, air, pride, plume, here
   Buckle! AND the fire that breaks from thee then, a billion
Times told lovelier, more dangerous, O my chevalier!

No wonder of it: shéer plód makes plough down sillion
Shine, and blue-bleak embers, ah my dear,
   Fall, gall themselves, and gash gold-vermilion.

Pied Beauty

Glory be to God for dappled things –
   For skies of couple-colour as a brinded cow;
     For rose-moles all in stipple upon trout that swim;
Fresh-firecoal chestnut-falls; finches' wings;
   Landscape plotted and pieced – fold, fallow, and plough;
     And áll trádes, their gear and tackle and trim.

All things counter, original, spare, strange;
   Whatever is fickle, freckled (who knows how?)
     With swift, slow; sweet, sour; adazzle, dim;
He fathers-forth whose beauty is past change:
                  Praise him.

The Caged Skylark

As a dare-gale skylark scanted in a dull cage
  Man's mounting spirit in his bone-house, mean house, dwells –
  That bird beyond the remembering his free fells,
This in drudgery, day-labouring-out life's age.

Though aloft on turf or perch or poor low stage,
  Both sing sometímes the sweetest, sweetest spells,
  Yet both droop deadly sómetimes in their cells
Or wring their barriers in bursts of fear or rage.

Not that the sweet-fowl, song-fowl, needs no rest –
Why, hear him, hear him babble and drop down to his nest,
  But his own nest, wild nest, no prison.

Man's spirit will be flesh-bound when found at best,
But uncumberèd: meadow-down is not distressed
  For a rainbow footing it nor he for his bónes rísen.

Hurrahing in Harvest

Summer ends now; now, barbarous in beauty, the stooks rise
Around; up above, what wind-walks! what lovely behaviour
Of silk-sack clouds! has wilder, wilful-wavier
Meal-drift moulded ever and melted across skies?

I walk, I lift up, I lift up heart, eyes,
Down all that glory in the heavens to glean our Saviour;
And, éyes, heárt, what looks, what lips yet gave you a
Rapturous love's greeting of realer, of rounder replies?

And the azurous hung hills are his world-wielding shoulder
Majestic – as a stallion stalwart, very-violet-sweet! –
These things, these things were here and but the beholder
Wanting; which two when they once meet,
The heart rears wings bold and bolder
And hurls for him, O half hurls earth for him off under his feet.

The Lantern out of Doors

Sometimes a lantern moves along the night.
   That interests our eyes. And who goes there?
   I think; where from and bound, I wonder, where,
With, all down darkness wide, his wading light?

Men go by me whom either beauty bright
   In mould or mind or what not else makes rare:
   They rain against our much-thick and marsh air
Rich beams, till death or distance buys them quite.

Death or distance soon consumes them: wind
   What most I may eye after, be in at the end
I cannot, and out of sight is out of mind.

Christ minds: Christ's interest, what to avow or amend
   There, éyes them, heart wánts, care haúnts, foot fóllows kínd,
Their ránsom, théir rescue, ánd first, fást, last friénd.

The Loss of the Eurydice

Foundered March 24, 1878

The Eurydice – it concerned thee, O Lord:
Three hundred souls, O alas! on board,
   Some asleep unawakened, all un-
warned, eleven fathoms fallen

Where she foundered! One stroke
Felled and furled them, the hearts of oak!
   And flockbells off the aerial
Downs' forefalls beat to the burial.   8

For did she pride her, freighted fully, on
Bounden bales or a hoard of bullion? –
   Precious passing measure,
Lads and men her lade and treasure.

She had come from a cruise, training seamen –
Men, boldboys soon to be men:
   Must it, worst weather,
Blast bole and bloom together?   16

No Atlantic squall overwrought her
Or rearing billow of the Biscay water:
   Home was hard at hand
And the blow bore from land.

And you were a liar, O blue March day.
Bright sun lanced fire in the heavenly bay;
   But what black Boreas wrecked her? he
Came equipped, deadly-electric,   24

A beetling baldbright cloud thorough England
Riding: there did storms not mingle? and
	Hailropes hustle and grind their
Heavengravel? wolfsnow, worlds of it, wind there?

Now Carisbrook keep goes under in gloom;
Now it overvaults Appledurcombe;
	Now near by Ventnor town
It hurls, hurls off Boniface Down.					32

Too proud, too proud, what a press she bore!
Royal, and all her royals wore.
	Sharp with her, shorten sail!
Too late; lost; gone with the gale.

This was that fell capsize.
As half she had righted and hoped to rise
	Death teeming in by her portholes
Raced down decks, round messes of mortals.				40

Then a lurch forward, frigate and men;
'All hands for themselves' the cry ran then;
	But she who had housed them thither
Was around them, bound them or wound them with her.

Marcus Hare, high her captain,
Kept to her – care-drowned and wrapped in
	Cheer's death, would follow
His charge through the champ-white water-in-a-wallow,		48

All under Channel to bury in a beach her
Cheeks: Right, rude of feature,
	He thought he heard say
'Her commander! and thou too, and thou this way.'

It is even seen, time's something server,
In mankind's medley a duty-swerver,
    At downright 'No or Yes?'
Doffs all, drives full for righteousness.   56

Sydney Fletcher, Bristol-bred,
(Low lie his mates now on watery bed)
    Takes to the seas and snows
As sheer down the ship goes.

Now her afterdraught gullies him too down;
Now he wrings for breath with the deathgush brown;
    Till a lifebelt and God's will
Lend him a lift from the sea-swill.   64

Now he shoots short up to the round air;
Now he gasps, now he gazes everywhere;
    But his eye no cliff, no coast or
Mark makes in the rivelling snowstorm.

Him, after an hour of wintry waves,
A schooner sights, with another, and saves,
    And he boards her in Oh! such joy
He has lost count what came next, poor boy. –   72

They say who saw one sea-corpse cold
He was all of lovely manly mould,
    Every inch a tar,
Of the best we boast our sailors are.

Look, foot to forelock, how all things suit! he
Is strung by duty, is strained to beauty,
    And brown-as-dawning-skinned
With brine and shine and whirling wind.   80

O his nimble finger, his gnarled grip!
Leagues, leagues of seamanship
    Slumber in these forsaken
Bones, this sinew, and will not waken.

He was but one like thousands more.
Day and night I deplore
    My people and born own nation,
Fast foundering own generation.   88

I might let bygones be – our curse
Of ruinous shrine no hand or, worse,
    Robbery's hand is busy to
Dress, hoar-hallowèd shrines unvisited;

Only the breathing temple and fleet
Life, this wildworth blown so sweet,
    These daredeaths, ay this crew, in
Unchrist, all rolled in ruin –   96

Deeply surely I need to deplore it,
Wondering why my master bore it,
    The riving off that race
So at home, time was, to his truth and grace

That a starlight-wender of ours would say
The marvellous Milk was Walsingham Way
    And one – but let be, let be:
More, more than was will yet be. –   104

O well wept, mother have lost son;
Wept, wife; wept, sweetheart would be one:
    Though grief yield them no good
Yet shed what tears sad truelove should.

But to Christ lord of thunder
Crouch; lay knee by earth low under:
    'Holiest, loveliest, bravest,
Save my hero, O Hero savest.   112

And the prayer thou hearst me making
Have, at the awful overtaking,
    Heard; have heard and granted
Grace that day grace was wanted.'

Not that hell knows redeeming,
But for souls sunk in seeming
    Fresh, till doomfire burn all,
Prayer shall fetch pity eternal.   120

The May Magnificat

May is Mary's month, and I
Muse at that and wonder why:
    Her feasts follow reason,
    Dated due to season –

Candlemas, Lady Day;
But the Lady Month, May,
    Why fasten that upon her,
    With a feasting in her honour?   8

Is it only its being brighter
Than the most are must delight her?
    Is it opportunest
    And flowers finds soonest?

Ask of her, the mighty mother:
Her reply puts this other
    Question: What is Spring? –
    Growth in every thing –   16

Flesh and fleece, fur and feather,
Grass and greenworld all together;
    Star-eyed strawberry-breasted
    Throstle above her nested

Cluster of bugle blue eggs thin
Forms and warms the life within;
    And bird and blossom swell
    In sod or sheath or shell.   24

All things rising, all things sizing
Mary sees, sympathising
    With that world of good,
    Nature's motherhood.

Their magnifying of each its kind
With delight calls to mind
    How she did in her stored
    Magnify the Lord.   32

Well but there was more than this:
Spring's universal bliss
    Much, had much to say
    To offering Mary May.

When drop-of-blood-and-foam-dapple
Bloom lights the orchard-apple
    And thicket and thorp are merry
    With silver-surfèd cherry   40

And azuring-over greybell makes
Wood banks and brakes wash wet like lakes
    And magic cuckoocall
    Caps, clears, and clinches all –

This ecstasy all through mothering earth
Tells Mary her mirth till Christ's birth
    To remember and exultation
    In God who was her salvation.   48

'The furl of fresh-leaved dogrose'

The furl of fresh-leaved dogrose down
His cheeks the forth-and-flaunting sun
Had swarthed about with lion-brown
    Before the Spring was done.
His locks like all a ravel-rope's-end,
    With hempen strands in spray –
Fallow, foam-fallow, hanks – fall'n off their ranks,
    Swung down at a disarray.

Or like a juicy and jostling shock
    Of bluebells sheaved in May
Or wind-long fleeces on the flock
    A day off shearing day.

Then over his turnèd temples – here –
    Was a rose, or, failing that,
Rough-Robin or five-lipped campion clear
    For a beauty-bow to his hat,
And the sunlight sidled, like dewdrops, like dandled diamonds

    Through the sieve of the straw of the plait.
    .   .   .   .

Binsey Poplars

felled 1879

My aspens dear, whose airy cages quelled,
Quelled or quenched in leaves the leaping sun,
All felled, felled, are all felled;
    Of a fresh and following folded rank
            Not spared, not one
            That dandled a sandalled
        Shadow that swam or sank
On meadow and river and wind-wandering weed-winding bank.   8

O if we but knew what we do
        When we delve or hew –
    Hack and rack the growing green!
        Since country is so tender
    To touch, her being só slender,
    That, like this sleek and seeing ball
    But a prick will make no eye at all,

Where we, even where we mean   16
            To mend her we end her,
        When we hew or delve:
After-comers cannot guess the beauty been.
    Ten or twelve, only ten or twelve
        Strokes of havoc únselve
            The sweet especial scene,
        Rural scene, a rural scene,
        Sweet especial rural scene.   24

Duns Scotus's Oxford

Towery city and branchy between towers;
Cuckoo-echoing, bell-swarmèd, lark-charmèd, rook-racked,
river-rounded;
The dapple-eared lily below thee; that country and town did
Once encounter in, here coped and poisèd powers;

Thou hast a base and brickish skirt there, sours
That neighbour-nature thy grey beauty is grounded
Best in; graceless growth, thou hast confounded
Rural rural keeping – folk, flocks, and flowers.

Yet ah! this air I gather and I release
He lived on; these weeds and waters, these walls are what
He haunted who of all men most sways my spirits to peace;

Of realty the rarest-veinèd unraveller; a not
Rivalled insight, be rival Italy or Greece;
Who fired France for Mary without spot.

Henry Purcell

The poet wishes well to the divine genius of Purcell and praises him that, whereas other musicians have given utterance to the moods of man's mind, he has, beyond that, uttered in notes the very make and species of man as created both in him and in all men generally.

Have fair fallen, O fair, fair have fallen, so dear
To me, so arch-especial a spirit as heaves in Henry Purcell,
An age is now since passed, since parted; with the reversal
Of the outward sentence low lays him, listed to a heresy, here.

Not mood in him nor meaning, proud fire or sacred fear,
Or love or pity or all that sweet notes not his might nursle:
It is the forgèd feature finds me; it is the rehearsal
Of own, of abrúpt sélf there so thrusts on, so throngs the ear.

Let him oh! with his air of angels then lift me, lay me! only I'll
Have an eye to the sakes of him, quaint moonmarks, to his pelted
                                                        plumage under
Wings: so some great stormfowl, whenever he has walked his while

The thunder-purple seabeach plumèd purple-of-thunder,
If a wuthering of his plamy snow-pinions scatter a colossal smile
Off him, but meaning motion fans fresh our wits with wonder.

The Candle Indoors

Some candle clear burns somewhere I come by.
I muse at how its being puts blissful back
With yellowy moisture mild night's blear-all black
Or to-fro tender trambeams truckle at the eye.

By that window what task what fingers ply,
I plod wondering, a-wanting, just for lack
Of answer the eagerer a-wanting Jessy or Jack
There / God to aggrándise, God to glorify. –

Come you indoors, come home; your fading fire
Mend first and vital candle in close heart's vault:
You there are master, do your own desire;

What hinders? Are you beam-blind, yet to a fault
In a neighbour deft-handed? Are you that liar
And, cast by conscience out, spendsavour salt?

The Handsome Heart:

at a Gracious Answer

'But tell me, child, your choice; what shall I buy
You?' – 'Father, what you buy me I like best.'
With the sweetest air that said, still plied and pressed,
He swung to his first poised purport of reply.

What the heart is! which, like carriers let fly –
Doff darkness, homing nature knows the rest –
To its own fine function, wild and self-instressed,
Falls light as ten years long taught how to and why.

Mannerly-hearted! more than handsome face –
Beauty's bearing or muse of mounting vein,
All, in this case, bathed in high hallowing grace . . .

Of heaven what boon to buy you, boy, or gain
Not granted? – Only . . . O on that path you pace
Run all your race, O brace sterner that strain!

The Bugler's First Communion

A bugler boy from barrack (it is over the hill
There) – boy bugler, born, he tells me, of Irish
    Mother to an English sire (he
Shares their best gifts surely, fall how things will),

This very very day came down to us after a boon he on
My late being there begged of me, overflowing
    Boon in my bestowing,
Came, I say, this day to it – to a First Communion.   8

Here he knelt then ín regimental red.
Forth Christ from cupboard fetched, how fain I of feet
    To his youngster take his treat!
Low-latched in leaf-light housel his too huge godhead.

There! and your sweetest sendings, ah divine,
By it, heavens, befall him! as a heart Christ's darling, dauntless;
    Tongue true, vaunt- and tauntless;
Breathing bloom of a chastity in mansex fine.   16

Frowning and forefending angel-warder
Squander the hell-rook ranks sally to molest him;
    March, kind comrade, abreast him;
Dress his days to a dexterous and starlight order.

How it dóes my heart good, visiting at that bleak hill,
When limber liquid youth, that to all I teach
    Yields tender as a pushed peach,
Hies headstrong to its wellbeing of a self-wise self-will!   24

Then though I should tread tufts of consolation
Dáys áfter, só I in a sort deserve to
          And do serve God to serve to
Just such slips of soldiery Christ's royal ration.

Nothing élse is like it, no, not all so strains
Us: freshyouth fretted in a bloomfall all portending
          That sweet's sweeter ending;
Realm both Christ is heir to and thére réigns.   32

O now well work that sealing sacred ointment!
O for now charms, arms, what bans off bad
          And locks love ever in a lad!
Let mé though see no more of him, and not disappointment

Those sweet hopes quell whose least me quickenings lift,
In scarlet or somewhere of some day seeing
          That brow and bead of being,
An our day's God's own Galahad. Though this child's drift   40

Seems by a divíne doom chánnelled, nor do I cry
Disaster there; but may he not rankle and roam
          In backwheels though bound home? –
That left to the Lord of the Eucharist, I here lie by;

Recorded only, I have put my lips on pleas
Would brandle adamantine heaven with ride and jar, did
          Prayer go disregarded:
Forward-like, but however, and like favourable heaven heard
                                                these.   48

Morning, Midday, and Evening Sacrifice

The dappled die-away
Cheek and the wimpled lip,
The gold-wisp, the airy-grey
Eye, all in fellowship –
This, all this beauty blooming,
This, all this freshness fuming,
Give God while worth consuming.

Both thought and thew now bolder
And told by Nature: Tower;
Head, heart, hand, heel, and shoulder
That beat and breathe in power –
This pride of prime's enjoyment
Take as for tool, not toy meant
And hold at Christ's employment.

The vault and scope and schooling
And mastery in the mind,
In silk-ash kept from cooling,
And ripest under rind –
What death half lifts the latch of,
What hell hopes soon the snatch of,
Your offering, with despatch, of!

35

Andromeda

Now Time's Andromeda on this rock rude,
With not her either beauty's equal or
Her injury's, looks off by both horns of shore,
Her flower, her piece of being, doomed dragon food.

Time past she has been attempted and pursued
By many blows and banes; but now hears roar
A wilder beast from West than all were, more
Rife in her wrongs, more lawless, and more lewd.

Her Perseus linger and leave her tó her extremes? –
Pillowy air he treads a time and hangs
His thoughts on her, forsaken that she seems,

All while her patience, morselled into pangs,
Mounts; then to alight disarming, no one dreams,
With Gorgon's gear and barebill / thongs and fangs.

Peace

When will you ever, Peace, wild wooddove, shy wings shut,
Your round me roaming end, and under be my boughs?
When, when, Peace, will you, Peace? – I'll not play hypocrite

To own my heart: I yield you do come sometimes; but
That piecemeal peace is poor peace. What pure peace allows
Alarms of wars, the daunting wars, the death of it?

O surely, reaving Peace, my Lord should leave in lieu
Some good! And so he does leave Patience exquisite,
That plumes to Peace thereafter. And when Peace here does house
He comes with work to do, he does not come to coo,
     He comes to brood and sit.

'As kingfishers catch fire'

As kingfishers catch fire, dragonflies draw flame;
   As tumbled over rim in roundy wells
   Stones ring; like each tucked string tells, each hung bell's
Bow swung finds tongue to fling out broad its name;
Each mortal thing does one thing and the same:
   Deals out that being indoors each one dwells;
   Selves – goes itself; *myself* it speaks and spells,
Crying *What I do is me: for that I came.*

Í say more: the just man justices;
   Keeps gráce: thát keeps all his goings graces;
Acts in God's eye what in God's eye he is –
   Chríst. For Christ plays in ten thousand places,
Lovely in limbs, and lovely in eyes not his
   To the Father through the features of men's faces.

At the Wedding March

God with honour hang your head,
Groom, and grace you, bride, your bed
With lissome scions, sweet scions,
Out of hallowed bodies bred.

Each be other's comfort kind:
Déep, déeper than divined,
Divine charity, dear charity,
Fast you ever, fast bind.

Then let the March tread our ears:
I to him turn with tears
Who to wedlock, his wonder wedlock,
Déals tríumph and immortal years.

Felix Randal

Felix Randal the farrier, O is he dead then? my duty all ended,
Who have watched his mould of man, big-boned and hardy-
                                                    handsome
Pining, pining, till time when reason rambled in it and some
Fatal four disorders, fleshed there, all contended?

Sickness broke him. Impatient, he cursed at first, but mended
Being anointed and all; though a heavenlier heart began some
Months earlier, since I had our sweet reprieve and ransom
Tendered to him. Ah well, God rest him all road ever he offended!

This seeing the sick endears them to us, us too it endears.
My tongue had taught thee comfort, touch had quenched thy tears,
Thy tears that touched my heart, child, Felix, poor Felix Randal;

How far from then forethought of, all thy more boisterous years,
When thou at the random grim forge, powerful amidst peers,
Didst fettle for the great grey drayhorse his bright and battering
                                                    sandal!

Brothers

How lovely the elder brother's
Life all laced in the other's,
Lóve-laced! – what once I well
Witnessed; so fortune fell.
When Shrovetide, two years gone,
Our boys' plays brought on
Part was picked for John,
Young Jóhn; then fear, then joy
Ran revel in the elder boy.
Now the night come; all   10
Our company thronged the hall;
Henry, by the wall,
Beckoned me beside him:
I came where called, and eyed him
By meanwhiles; making mý play
Turn most on tender byplay.
For, wrung all on love's rack,
My lad, and lost in Jack,
Smiled, blushed, and bit his lip;
Or drove, with a diver's dip,   20
Clutched hands through claspèd knees;
And many a mark like these,
Told tales with what heart's stress
He hung on the imp's success.
Now the other was bráss-bóld:
Hé had no work to hold
His heart up at the strain;
Nay, roguish ran the vein.
Two tedious acts were past;
Jack's call and cue at last;   30
When Henry, heart-forsook,

Dropped eyes and dared not look.
Thére! the háll rúng!
Dog, he did give tongue!
But Harry – in his hands he has flung
His tear-tricked cheeks of flame
For fond love and for shame.
  Ah Nature, framed in fault,
There's comfort then, there's salt;
Nature, bad, base, and blind,   40
Dearly thou canst be kind;
There dearly thén, deárly,
Dearly thou canst be kind.

Spring and Fall:

to a young child

Márgarét, áre you gríeving
Over Goldengrove unleaving?
Leáves, líke the things of man, you
With your fresh thoughts care for, can you?
Áh! ás the heart grows older
It will come to such sights colder
By and by, nor spare a sigh
Though worlds of wanwood leafmeal lie;
And yet you *will* weep and know why.
Now no matter, child, the name:
Sórrow's spríngs áre the same.
Nor mouth had, no nor mind, expressed
What heart heard of, ghost guessed:
It ís the blight man was born for,
It is Margaret you mourn for.

Inversnaid

This darksome burn, horseback brown,
His rollrock highroad roaring down,
In coop and in comb the fleece of his foam
Flutes and low to the lake falls home.

A windpuff-bonnet of fáwn-fróth
Turns and twindles over the broth
Of a pool so pitchblack, féll-frówning,
It rounds and rounds Despair to drowning.

Degged with dew, dappled with dew
Are the groins of the braes that the brook treads through,
Wiry heathpacks, flitches of fern,
And the beadbonny ash that sits over the burn.

What would the world be, once bereft
Of wet and of wildness? Let them be left,
O let them be left, wildness and wet;
Long live the weeds and the wilderness yet.

Ribblesdale

Earth, sweet Earth, sweet landscape, with leavès throng
And louchèd low grass, heaven that dost appeal
To, with no tongue to plead, no heart to feel;
That canst but only be, but dost that long –

Thou canst but be, but that thou well dost; strong
Thy plea with him who dealt, nay does now deal,
Thy lovely dale down thus and thus bids reel
Thy river, and o'er gives all to rack or wrong.

And what is Earth's eye, tongue, or heart else, where
Else, but in dear and dogged man? – Ah, the heir
To his own selfbent so bound, so tied to his turn,

To thriftless reave both our rich round world bare
And none reck of world after, this bids wear
Earth brows of such care, care and dear concern.

The Leaden Echo and the Golden Echo

(Maidens' song from St Winefred's Well)

THE LEADEN ECHO

How to kéep – is there ány any, is there none such, nowhere
    known some, bow or brooch or braid or brace, láce, latch or
        catch or key to keep
Back beauty, keep it, beauty, beauty, beauty, . . . from vanishing
        away?
Ó is there no frowning of these wrinkles, rankèd wrinkles deep,
Dówn? no waving off of these most mournful messengers, still
        messengers, sad and stealing messengers of grey? –
No there's none, there's none, O no there's none,
Nor can you long be, what you now are, called fair,
Do what you may do, what, do what you may,
And wisdom is early to despair: 8
Be beginning; since, no, nothing can be done
To keep at bay
Age and age's evils, hoar hair,
Ruck and wrinkle, drooping, dying, death's worst, winding sheets,
        tombs and worms and tumbling to decay;
So be beginning, be beginning to despair.
O there's none; no no no there's none:
Be beginning to despair, to despair,
Despair, despair, despair, despair.   16

THE GOLDEN ECHO

        Spare!
There ís one, yes I have one (Hush there!),
Only not within seeing of the sun.
Not within the singeing of the strong sun,

Tall sun's tingeing, or treacherous the tainting of the earth's air,
Somewhere elsewhere there is ah well where! one,
Óne. Yes I cán tell such a key, I dó know such a place,
Where whatever's prizèd and passes of us, everything that's fresh
         and fast flying of us, seems to us sweet of us and swiftly
                  away with, done away with, undone, 8
Undone, done with, soon done with, and yet dearly and
                                dangerously sweet
Of us, the wimpled-water-dimpled, not-by-morning-matchèd face,
The flower of beauty, fleece of beauty, too too apt to, ah! to fleet,
Never fleets móre, fastened with the tenderest truth
To its own best being and its loveliness of youth: it is an ever-
                    lastingness of, O it is an all youth!
Come then, your ways and airs and looks, locks, maidengear,
                  gallantry and gaiety and grace,
Winning ways, airs innocent, maiden manners, sweet looks, loose
    locks, long locks, lovelocks, gaygear, going gallant, girlgrace –
Resign them, sign them, seal them, send them, motion them with
                        breath, 16
And with sighs soaring, soaring síghs, deliver
Them; beauty-in-the-ghost, deliver it, early now, long before death
Give beauty back, beauty, beauty, beauty, back to God, beauty's
                  self and beauty's giver.
See; not a hair is, not an eyelash, not the least lash lost; every hair
Is, hair of the head, numbered.
Nay, what we had lighthanded left in surly the mere mould
Will have waked and have waxed and have walked with the wind
                  what while we slept,
This side, that side hurling a heavyheaded hundredfold 24
What while we, while we slumbered.
O then, weary then whý should we tread? O why are we so
    haggard at the heart, so care-coiled, care-killed, so fagged, so
                fashed, so cogged, so cumbered,
When the thing we freely fórfeit is kept with fonder a care,
Fonder a care kept than we could have kept it, kept

Far with fonder a care (and we, we should have lost it) finer, fonder
A care kept. – Where kept? do but tell us where kept, where. –
Yonder. – What high as that! We follow, now we follow. –

Yonder, yes yonder, yonder,
Yonder.
32

The Blessed Virgin compared to the Air we Breathe

Wild air, world-mothering air,
Nestling me everywhere,
That each eyelash or hair
Girdles; goes home betwixt
The fleeciest, frailest-flixed
Snowflake; that's fairly mixed
With, riddles, and is rife
In every least thing's life;
This needful, never spent,
And nursing element;   10
My more than meat and drink,
My meal at every wink;
This air, which, by life's law,
My lung must draw and draw
Now but to breathe its praise,
Minds me in many ways
Of her who not only
Gave God's infinity
Dwindled to infancy
Welcome in womb and breast,   20
Birth, milk, and all the rest
But mothers each new grace
That does now reach our race –
Mary Immaculate,
Merely a woman, yet
Whose presence, power is
Great as no goddess's
Was deemèd, dreamèd; who
This one work has to do –

Let all God's glory through,   30
God's glory which would go
Through her and from her flow
Off, and no way but so.
    I say that we are wound
With mercy round and round
As if with air: the same
Is Mary, more by name.
She, wild web, wondrous robe,
Mantles the guilty globe,
Since God has let dispense   40
Her prayers his providence:
Nay, more than almoner,
The sweet alms' self is her
And men are meant to share
Her life as life does air.
    If I have understood,
She holds high motherhood
Towards all our ghostly good
And plays in grace her part
About man's beating heart,   50
Laying, like air's fine flood,
The deathdance in his blood;
Yet no part but what will
Be Christ our Saviour still.
Of her flesh he took flesh:
He does take fresh and fresh,
Though much the mystery how,
Not flesh but spirit now
And makes, O marvellous!
New Nazareths in us,   60
Where she shall yet conceive
Him, morning, noon, and eve;
New Bethlems, and he born
There, evening, noon, and morn –

Bethlem or Nazareth,
Men here may draw like breath
More Christ and baffle death;
Who, born so, comes to be
New self and nobler me
In each one and each one   70
More makes, when all is done,
Both God's and Mary's Son.
    Again, look overhead
How air is azurèd;
O how! Nay do but stand
Where you can lift your hand
Skywards: rich, rich it laps
Round the four fingergaps.
Yet such a sapphire-shot,
Charged, steepèd sky will not   80
Stain light. Yea, mark you this:
It does no prejudice.
The glass-blue days are those
When every colour glows,
Each shape and shadow shows.
Blue be it: this blue heaven
The seven or seven times seven
Hued sunbeam will transmit
Perfect, not alter it.
Or if there does some soft,   90
On things aloof, aloft,
Bloom breathe, that one breath more
Earth is the fairer for.
Whereas did air not make
This bath of blue and slake
His fire, the sun would shake,
A blear and blinding ball
With blackness bound, and all
The thick stars round him roll

Flashing like flecks of coal,
Quartz-fret, or sparks of salt,
In grimy vasty vault.
 So God was god of old:
A mother came to mould
Those limbs like ours which are
What must make our daystar
Much dearer to mankind;
Whose glory bare would blind
Or less would win man's mind.
Through her we may see him
Made sweeter, not made dim,
And her hand leaves his light
Sifted to suit our sight.
 Be thou then, O thou dear
Mother, my atmosphere;
My happier world, wherein
To wend and meet no sin;
Above me, round me lie
Fronting my froward eye
With sweet and scarless sky;
Stir in my ears, speak there
Of God's love, O live air,
Of patience, penance, prayer:
Worldmothering air, air wild,
Wound with thee, in thee isled,
Fold home, fast fold thy child.

'The times are nightfall'

The times are nightfall, look, their light grows less;
The times are winter, watch, a world undone:
They waste, they wither worse; they as they run
Or bring more or more blazon man's distress.
And I not help. Nor word now of success:
All is from wreck, here, there, to rescue one –
Work which to see scarce so much as begun
Makes welcome death, does dear forgetfulness.

Or what is else? There is your world within.
There rid the dragons, root out there the sin.
Your will is law in that small commonweal.

. . . .

Spelt from Sibyl's Leaves

Earnest, earthless, equal, attuneable, ' vaulty, voluminous,
. . . stupendous
Evening strains to be tíme's vást, ' womb-of-all, home-of-all,
hearse-of-all night.
Her fond yellow hornlight wound to the west, ' her wild hollow
hoarlight hung to the height
Waste; her earliest stars, earlstars, ' stárs principal, overbend us,
Fíre-féaturing héaven. For éarth ' her béing has unbóund; her
dápple is at énd, as-
Tray or aswarm, all throughther, in throngs; ' self ín self stéepèd
and páshed – qúite
Disremembering, dísmémbering ' áll now. Heart, you round me
right
With: Óur évening is óver us; óur night ' whélms, whélms, ánd
will énd us.
Only the beakleaved boughs dragonish ' damask the tool-smooth
bleak light; black,
Ever so black on it. Óur tale, O óur oracle! ' Lét life, wáned, ah
lét life wínd
Off hér once skéined stained véined varíety ' upon, áll on twó
spools; párt, pen, páck
Now her áll in twó flocks, twó folds – bláck, white; ' ríght, wrong;
réckon but, réck but, mínd
But thése two; wáre of a wórld where bút these ' twó tell, éach off
the óther; of a ráck
Where, selfwrung, selfstrung, sheathe-and shelterless, ' thóughts
agaínst thoughts ín groans grínd.

'Thee, God, I come from'

Thee, God, I come from, to thee go,
All dáy long I like fountain flow
From thy hand out, swayed about
Mote-like in thy mighty glow.

What I know of thee I bless,
As acknowledging thy stress
On my being and as seeing
Something of thy holiness.   8

Once I turned from thee and hid,
Bound on what thou hadst forbid;
Sow the wind I would; I sinned:
I repent of what I did.

Bad I am, but yet thy child.
Father, be thou reconciled.
Spare thou me, since I see
With thy might that thou art mild.   16

I have life left with me still
And thy purpose to fulfil;
Yea a debt to pay thee yet:
Help me, sir, and so I will.

But thou bidst, and just thou art,
Me shew mercy from my heart
Towards my brother, every other
Man my mate and counterpart.   24

.   .   .   .   .   .

To what serves Mortal Beauty?

To what serves mortal beauty ' – dangerous; does set danc-
ing blood – the O-seal-that-so ' feature, flung prouder form
Than Purcell tune lets tread to? ' See: it does this: keeps warm
Men's wits to the things that are; ' what good means – where a
                                                                glance
Master more may than gaze, ' gaze out of countenance.
Those lovely lads once, wet-fresh ' windfalls of war's storm,
How then should Gregory, a father, ' have gleanèd else from
                                                                swarm-
èd Rome? But God to a nation ' dealt that day's dear chance.
To man, that needs would worship ' block or barren stone,
Our law says: Love what are ' love's worthiest, were all known;
World's loveliest – men's selves. Self ' flashes off frame and face.
What do then? how meet beauty? ' Merely meet it; own,
Home at heart, heaven's sweet gift; ' then leave, let that alone.
Yea, wish that though, wish all, ' God's better beauty, grace.

50

[The Soldier]

Yes. Whý do we áll, seeing of a soldier, bless him? bless
Our redcoats, our tars? Both these being, the greater part,
But frail clay, nay but foul clay. Here it is: the heart,
Since, proud, it calls the calling manly, gives a guess
That, hopes that, makesbelieve, the men must be no less;
It fancies, feigns, deems, dears the artist after his art;
And fain will find as sterling all as all is smart,
And scarlet wear the spirit of wár thére express.
Mark Christ our King. He knows war, served this soldiering
through;
He of all can reeve a rope best. There he bides in bliss
Now, and séeing somewhére some mán do all that man can do,
For love he leans forth, needs his neck must fall on, kiss,
And cry 'O Christ-done deed! So God-made-flesh does too:
Were I come o'er again' cries Christ 'it should be this'.

'What shall I do for the land'

What shall I do for the land that bred me,
Her homes and fields that folded and fed me?
Be under her banner and live for her honour:
Under her banner I'll live for her honour.
 CHORUS. Under her banner we live for her honour.

Not the pleasure, the pay, the plunder,
But country and flag, the flag I am under –
There is the shilling that finds me willing
To follow a banner and fight for honour.
 CH. We follow her banner, we fight for her honour.

Call me England's fame's fond lover,
Her fame to keep, her fame to recover.
Spend me or end me what God shall send me,
But under her banner I live for her honour.
 CH. Under her banner we march for her honour.

Where is the field I must play the man on?
O welcome there their steel or cannon.
Immortal beauty is death with duty,
If under her banner I fall for her honour.
 CH. Under her banner we fall for her honour.

[Carrion Comfort]

Not, I'll not, carrion comfort, Despair, not feast on thee;
Not untwist – slack they may be – these last strands of man
In me ór, most weary, cry *I can no more*. I can;
Can something, hope, wish day come, not choose not to be.

But ah, but O thou terrible, why wouldst thou rude on me
Thy wring-world right foot rock? lay a lionlimb against me? scan
With darksome devouring eyes my bruisèd bones? and fan,
O in turns of tempest, me heaped there; me frantic to avoid thee
                                                                                    and flee?

Why? That my chaff might fly; my grain lie, sheer and clear.
Nay in all that toil, that coil, since (seems) I kissed the rod,
Hand rather, my heart lo! lapped strength, stole joy, would laugh,
                                                                                    chéer.
Cheer whom though? The hero whose heaven-handling flung me,
                                                                                    fóot tród
Me? or me that fought him? O which one? is it each one? That
                                                                                    night, that year
Of now done darkness I wretch lay wrestling with (my God!) my
                                                                                    God.

'No worst, there is none'

No worst, there is none. Pitched past pitch of grief,
More pangs will, schooled at forepangs, wilder wring.
Comforter, where, where is your comforting?
Mary, mother of us, where is your relief?
My cries heave, herds-long; huddle in a main, a chief-
woe, world-sorrow; on an age-old anvil wince and sing –
Then lull, then leave off. Fury had shrieked 'No ling-
ering! Let me be fell: force I must be brief'.
O the mind, mind has mountains; cliffs of fall
Frightful, sheer, no-man-fathomed. Hold them cheap
May who ne'er hung there. Nor does long our small
Durance deal with that steep or deep. Here! creep,
Wretch, under a comfort serves in a whirlwind: all
Life death does end and each day dies with sleep.

'To seem the stranger'

To seem the stranger lies my lot, my life
Among strangers. Father and mother dear,
Brothers and sisters are in Christ not near
And he my peace / my parting, sword and strife.

England, whose honour O all my heart woos, wife
To my creating thought, would neither hear
Me, were I pleading, plead nor do I: I wear-
y of idle a being but by where wars are rife.

I am in Ireland now; now I am at a third
Remove. Not but in all removes I can
Kind love both give and get. Only what word

Wisest my heart breeds dark heaven's baffling ban
Bars or hell's spell thwarts. This to hoard unheard,
Heard unheeded, leaves me a lonely began.

'I wake and feel the fell of dark'

I wake and feel the fell of dark, not day.
What hours, O what black hoürs we have spent
This night! what sights you, heart, saw; ways you went!
And more must, in yet longer light's delay.

With witness I speak this. But where I say
Hours I mean years, mean life. And my lament
Is cries countless, cries like dead letters sent
To dearest him that lives alas! away.

I am gall, I am heartburn. God's most deep decree
Bitter would have me taste: my taste was me;
Bones built in me, flesh filled, blood brimmed the curse.

Selfyeast of spirit a dull dough sours. I see
The lost are like this, and their scourge to be
As I am mine, their sweating selves; but worse.

'Patience, hard thing!'

Patience, hard thing! the hard thing but to pray,
But bid for, Patience is! Patience who asks
Wants war, wants wounds; weary his times, his tasks;
To do without, take tosses, and obey.

Rare patience roots in these, and, these away,
Nowhere. Natural heart's ivy, Patience masks
Our ruins of wrecked past purpose. There she basks
Purple eyes and seas of liquid leaves all day.

We hear our hearts grate on themselves: it kills
To bruise them dearer. Yet the rebellious wills
Of us we do bid God bend to him even so.

And where is he who more and more distills
Delicious kindness? – He is patient. Patience fills
His crisp combs, and that comes those ways we know.

'My own heart let me more have pity on'

My own heart let me more have pity on; let
Me live to my sad self hereafter kind,
Charitable; not live this tormented mind
With this tormented mind tormenting yet.

I cast for comfort I can no more get
By groping round my comfortless, than blind
Eyes in their dark can day or thirst can find
Thirst's all-in-all in all a world of wet.

Soul, self; come, poor Jackself, I do advise
You, jaded, let be; call off thoughts awhile
Elsewhere; leave comfort root-room; let joy size

At God knows when to God knows what; whose smile
's not wrung, see you; unforeseen times rather – as skies
Betweenpie mountains – lights a lovely mile.

[Ashboughs]

Not of all my eyes see, wandering on the world,
Is anything a milk to the mind so, so sighs deep
Poetry tó it, as a tree whose boughs break in the sky.
Say it is áshboughs: whether on a December day and furled
Fast ór they in clammyish lashtender combs creep
Apart wide and new-nestle at heaven most high.

They touch heaven, tabour on it; how their talons sweep
The smouldering enormous winter welkin! May
Mells blue and snowwhite through them, a fringe and fray
Of greenery: it is old earth's groping towards the steep
Heaven whom she childs us by.

On the Portrait of Two Beautiful Young People

A Brother and Sister

O I admire and sorrow! The heart's eye grieves
Discovering you, dark tramplers, tyrant years.
A juice rides rich through bluebells, in vine leaves,
And beauty's dearest veriest vein is tears.

Happy the father, mother of these! Too fast:
Not that, but thus far, all with frailty, blest
In one fair fall; but, for time's aftercast,
Creatures all heft, hope, hazard, interest.   8

And are they thus? The fine, the fingering beams
Their young delightful hour do feature down
That fleeted else like day-dissolvèd dreams
Or ringlet-race on burling Barrow brown.

She leans on him with such contentment fond
As well the sister sits, would well the wife;
His looks, the soul's own letters, see beyond,
Gaze on, and fall directly forth on life.   16

But ah, bright forelock, cluster that you are
Of favoured make and mind and health and youth,
Where lies your landmark, seamark, or soul's star?
There's none but truth can stead you. Christ is truth.

There's none but good can bé good, both for you
And what sways with you, maybe this sweet maid;
None good but God – a warning wavèd to
One once that was found wanting when Good weighed.   24

Man lives that list, that leaning in the will
No wisdom can forecast by gauge or guess,
The selfless self of self, most strange, most still,
Fast furled and all foredrawn to No or Yes.

Your feast of; that most in you earnest eye
May but call on your banes to more carouse.   30
Worst will the best. What worm was here, we cry,
To have havoc-pocked so, see the hung-heavenward boughs?

Enough: corruption was the world's first woe.
What need I strain my heart beyond my ken?
O but I bear my burning witness though
Against the wild and wanton work of men.

·   ·   ·   ·   ·   ·   ·   ·

Harry Ploughman

Hard as hurdle arms, with a broth of goldish flue
Breathed round; the rack of ribs; the scooped flank; lank
Rope-over thigh; knee-nave; and barrelled shank –
        Head and foot, shoulder and shank –
By a grey eye's heed steered well, one crew, fall to;
Stand at stress. Each limb's barrowy brawn, his thew
That onewhere curded, onewhere sucked or sank –
        Soared ór sánk –,
Though as a beechbole firm, finds his, as at a rollcall, rank
And features, in flesh, what deed he each must do –
        His sinew-service where do.
He leans to it, Harry bends, look. Back, elbow, and liquid waist
In him, all quail to the wallowing o' the plough. 'S cheek crimsons;
        curls
Wag or crossbridle, in a wind lifted, windlaced –
        See his wind- lilylocks -laced;
Churlsgrace too, child of Amansstrength, how it hangs or hurls
Them – broad in bluff hide his frowning feet lashed! raced
With, along them, cragiron under and cold furls –
        With-a-fountain's shining-shot furls.

Tom's Garland:

upon the Unemployed

Tom – garlanded with squat and surly steel
Tom; then Tom's fallowbootfellow piles pick
By him and rips out rockfire homeforth – sturdy Dick;
Tom Heart-at-ease, Tom Navvy: he is all for his meal
Sure, 's bed now. Low be it: lustily he his low lot (feel
That ne'er need hunger, Tom; Tom seldom sick,
Seldomer heartsore; that treads through, prickproof, thick
Thousands of thorns, thoughts) swings though. Commonweal   8
Little Í reck ho! lacklevel in, if all had bread:
What! Country is honour enough in all us – lordly head,
With heaven's lights high hung round, or, mother-ground
That mammocks, mighty foot. But nó way sped,
Nor mind nor mainstrength; gold go garlanded
With, perilous, O nó; nor yet plod safe shod sound;
    Undenizened, beyond bound
Of earth's glory, earth's ease, all; no one, nowhere,   16
In wide the world's weal; rare gold, bold steel, bare
   In both; care, but share care –
This, by Despair, bred Hangdog dull; by Rage,
Manwolf, worse; and their packs infest the age.

Epithalamion

Hark, hearer, hear what I do; lend a thought now, make believe
We are leafwhelmed somewhere with the hood
Of some branchy bunchy bushybowered wood,
Southern dean or Lancashire clough or Devon cleave,
That leans along the loins of hills, where a candycoloured, where
a gluegold-brown
Marbled river, boisterously beautiful, between
Roots and rocks is danced and dandled, all in froth and water-
blowballs, down.
We are there, when we hear a shout
That the hanging honeysuck, the dogeared hazels in the cover
Makes dither, makes hover   10
And the riot of a rout
Of, it must be, boys from the town
Bathing: it is summer's sovereign good.

By there comes a listless stranger: beckoned by the noise
He drops towards the river: unseen
Sees the bevy of them, how the boys
With dare and with downdolphinry and bellright bodies huddling
out,
Are earthworld, airworld, waterworld thorough hurled, all by turn
and turn about.

This garland of their gambol flashes in his breast
Into such a sudden zest   20
Of summertime joys
That he hies to a pool neighbouring; sees it is the best
There; sweetest, freshest, shadowiest;
Fairyland; silk-beech, scrolled ash, packed sycamore, wild wychelm,
hornbeam fretty overstood

By. Rafts and rafts of flake leaves light, dealt so, painted on the air,
Hang as still as hawk or hawkmoth, as the stars or as the angels
there,
Like the thing that never knew the earth, never off roots
Rose. Here he feasts: lovely all is! No more: off with – down he
dings
His bleachèd both and woolwoven wear:
Careless these in coloured wisp   30
All lie tumbled-to; then with loop-locks
Forward falling, forehead frowning, lips crisp
Over finger-teasing task, his twiny boots
Fast he opens, last he off wrings
Till walk the world he can with bare his feet
And come where lies a coffer, burly all of blocks
Built of chancequarrièd, selfquainèd, hoar-huskèd rocks
And the water warbles over into, filleted ¹ with glassy grassy
quicksilvery shivès and shoots
And with heavenfallen freshness down from moorland still brims,
Dark or daylight on and on. Here he will then, here he will the
fleet 40
Flinty kindcold element let break across his limbs
Long. Where we leave him, froliclavish, while he looks about him,
laughs, swims.

Enough now; since the sacred matter that I mean
I should be wronging longer leaving it to float
Upon this only gambolling and echoing-of-earth note –

What is . . . . the delightful dean?
Wedlock. What the water? Spousal love.

            •   •   •   •   •   •   •   •   •

     .   .   .   .

                         turns

Father, mother, brothers, sisters, friends
Into fairy trees, wildflowers, woodferns   50
Rankèd round the bower

      .   .   .   .   .   .

63

That Nature is a Heraclitean Fire and of the comfort of the Resurrection

Cloud-puffball, torn tufts, tossed pillows ¹ flaunt forth, then chevy
on an air-
built thoroughfare: heaven-roysterers, in gay-gangs ¹ they throng;
they glitter in marches.
Down roughcast, down dazzling whitewash, ¹ wherever an elm
arches,
Shivelights and shadowtackle in long ¹ lashes lace, lance, and pair.
Delightfully the bright wind boisterous ¹ ropes, wrestles, beats
earth bare
Of yestertempest's creases; ¹ in pool and rutpeel parches
Squandering ooze to squeezed ¹ dough, crust, dust; stanches,
starches
Squadroned masks and manmarks ¹ treadmire toil there   8
Footfretted in it. Million-fuelèd, ¹ nature's bonfire burns on.
But quench her bonniest, dearest ¹ to her, her clearest-selvèd spark
Man, how fast his firedint, ¹ his mark on mind, is gone!
Both are in an unfathomable, all is in an enormous dark
Drowned. O pity and indig ¹ nation! Manshape, that shone
Sheer off, disseveral, a star, ¹ death blots black out; nor mark
Is any of him at all so stark
But vastness blurs and time ¹ beats level. Enough! the
Resurrection,   16
A heart's-clarion! Away grief's gasping, ¹ joyless days, dejection.
Across my foundering deck shone
A beacon, an eternal beam. ¹ Flesh fade, and mortal trash
Fall to the residuary worm; ¹ world's wildfire, leave but ash:
In a flash, at a trumpet crash,
I am all at once what Christ is, ¹ since he was what I am, and

This Jack, joke, poor potsherd, ¹ patch, matchwood, immortal
diamond,
Is immortal diamond.   24

64

In honour of

St Alphonsus Rodriguez

Laybrother of the Society of Jesus

Honour is flashed off exploit, so we say;
And those strokes once that gashed flesh or galled shield
Should tongue that time now, trumpet now that field,
And, on the fighter, forge his glorious day.
On Christ they do and on the martyr may;
But be the war within, the brand we wield
Unseen, the heroic breast not outward-steeled,
Earth hears no hurtle then from fiercest fray.
Yet God (that hews mountain and continent,
Earth, all, out; who, with trickling increment,
Veins violets and tall trees makes more and more)
Could crowd career with conquest while there went
Those years and years by of world without event
That in Majorca Alfonso watched the door.

65

'Thou art indeed just, Lord'

*Justus quidem tu es, Domine, si disputem tecum; verumtamen
justa loquar ad te: Quare via impiorum prosperatur? &c.*

Thou art indeed just, Lord, if I contend
With thee; but, sir, so what I plead is just.
Why do sinners' ways prosper? and why must
Disappointment all I endeavour end?

Wert thou my enemy, O thou my friend,
How wouldst thou worse, I wonder, than thou dost
Defeat, thwart me? Oh, the sots and thralls of lust
Do in spare hours more thrive than I that spend,

Sir, life upon thy cause. See, banks and brakes
Now, leavèd how thick! lacèd they are again
With fretty chervil, look, and fresh wind shakes

Them; birds build – but not I build; no, but strain,
Time's eunuch, and not breed one work that wakes.
Mine, O thou lord of life, send my roots rain.

'The shepherd's brow'

The shepherd's brow, fronting forked lightning, owns
The horror and the havoc and the glory
Of it. Angels fall, they are towers, from heaven – a story
Of just, majestical, and giant groans.
But man – we, scaffold of score brittle bones;
Who breathe, from groundlong babyhood to hoary
Age gasp; whose breath is our *memento mori* –
What bass is *our* viol for tragic tones?
He! Hand to mouth he lives, and voids with shame;
And, blazoned in however bold the name,
Man Jack the man is, just; his mate a hussy.
And I that die these deaths, that feed this flame,
That . . . in smooth spoons spy life's masque mirrored: tame
My tempests there, my fire and fever fussy.

To R.B.

The fine delight that fathers thought; the strong
Spur, live and lancing like the blowpipe flame,
Breathes once and, quenchèd faster than it came,
Leaves yet the mind a mother of immortal song.

Nine months she then, nay years, nine years she long
Within her wears, bears, cares and combs the same:
The widow of an insight lost she lives, with aim
Now known and hand at work now never wrong.

Sweet fire the sire of muse, my soul needs this;
I want the one rapture of an inspiration.
O then if in my lagging lines you miss

The roll, the rise, the carol, the creation,
My winter world, that scarcely breathes that bliss
Now, yields you, with some sighs, our explanation.

Notes

N.B. Before using these Notes, readers are urged to consult the Introduction, especially marking the cautions on pp. 10, 11 and 23.

1 *A Windy Day in Summer*

'I have been writing numbers of descriptions of sunrises, sunsets, sunlight in the trees, flowers, windy skies etc. etc.', Hopkins told his school friend E. H. Coleridge (grandson of the famous poet) in a letter of 3 September 1862. This is one of his earliest surviving pieces, composed before he entered his last year at Highgate school.

2 *Heaven-Haven*
3 *'I must hunt down the prize'*

July 1864. These embody opposite moods – retreat and Ulysses-like adventurousness.

4 *See how Spring opens*

26 June 1865. This speaks of his religious perplexities, and foreshadows his conversion to the Catholic Church.

5 *The Nightingale*

18–19 January 1866. Included here as an example of a narrative love poem, put into the mouth of a woman. It is curious that this romantic monologue should bear exactly the same date as the austere religious poem which follows it, No. 6.

6 *The Habit of Perfection*

18–19 January 1866. Mystical paradoxes underlie this beautiful lyric, written while he was still in the Church of England, six months before he had decided that he could not remain a member of it. (See Introduction pp. 10–11.)

l.2; *whorlèd*: shell-shaped, coiled.
l.6; *the shut*: closure (usually in 'the shut of day').
l.11; *this ruck and reel*: these crowds and confusion.
l.12; *Coils, keeps, and teases*: snares, engrosses, and distracts.
l.18; *stir and keep*: creation and upkeep.
l.24; *unhouse . . . the Lord*: take the consecrated elements of the communion from the altar tabernacle.
ll.27–8: Poverty is called on to provide her bridegroom with the robes of

righteousness, white as the liles; *cf. Matthew* 6:28–33 and *Revelation* 19:7–8.

7 *Nondum*

Lent 1866. Nineteenth century scientific discoveries had led to wide-spread agnosticism. In this dignified and highly imaginative projection of Victorian doubts, the poet addresses a Lord of creation in whose existence many had ceased to believe. He writes as a man whose faith is dying, since he cannot yet claim either external proof or inner reassurance. (The Latin title means 'Not Yet'.) Note the intensification of feeling as the 'we' of the earlier portion changes to 'I' from *st.* 7 onwards.

8 *Jesu Dulcis Memoria*

Undated. This is a translation of an ancient Latin hymn, the commoner version of which is based on a Primer of 1706: 'Jesus, the very thought of Thee'. Hopkins had by the time he wrote this found full assurance in the Catholic Church.

9 *The Wreck of the Deutschland*

1875–76. *Introductory.* In December 1875 the iron-clad single-screw steamer the 'Deutschland' (2751 British tons gross, 328 feet long, with a 40-foot beam) set out from Bremerhaven in Germany for New York, with a crew of 99 and about 113 passengers, including five nuns whose cloister had been closed by government edict. Hurried on her voyage through the treacherous North Sea by a following gale, she veered off course in the dark, snowstorms and haze preventing the master from checking his position. Shortly after 5 a.m. there was a cry of 'Breakers ahead!' The engines were immediately reversed but the screw broke, and the prow became embedded on a submerged sandbank, lifting and crashing down 'with ruinous shock' as successive waves drove her further and further on to the sands. The men of the Kentish Knock Lightship, only two-and-a-half miles away, did not see her until over four hours later, so terrible was the weather, and guns which were fired to report the disaster to Harwich (followed by rockets after dark) brought them no rescue. In the teeth of that gale the coastguards at Harwich could not launch a lifeboat. During the second night the tide rose over 20 feet, flooding the cabins and saloons, and forcing the survivors into the rigging. All the ship's lifeboats but one were smashed or swamped. From the freezing shrouds many fell numbed into the swirling sea below. Before a rescue vessel could reach them, 29 hours after the stranding, some 60 lives had been lost, including all five of the Franciscan nuns.

The story of the wreck and of the role played by the tall leader of the nuns stirred Hopkins from the poetic silence in which he had lived almost entirely since he had entered the Society of Jesus, seven years earlier.

Part the First is a personal prologue to his ode on the wreck: it is more easily understood after a reading of Part the Second, when its many parallels will be apparent. The poet begins with a recognition (in gratitude mixed with fear) of God's mastery over his own life, recalling his summons to serve Him and the renewal of his submission now, as he has been touched by the account of the sisters' faith (*sts.* 1–3). He considers the close affinity between divine power and mercy, one being the obverse of the other, though the evidence in storm and lightning of God's omnipotence seems to contrast so strongly with the inflooding sense of His warmth and beauty which pulses out from a starlit sky or a colour-dappled sunset (*st.* 5). He recognises Christ's incarnation and sacrifice as the origin of men's awareness of God's love – His 'stress' (*sts.* 6–8). The poet's prayer is that whether by rough means or gentle Christ may win all men to obedience: 'Make mercy in all of us, out of us all/Mastery'. This first movement thus ends as it began with emphasis upon God as the Master – a title, ironically, claimed by the captain of every wrecked ship.

Part the Second. The poet retells the story in magnificent verse (*sts.* 12–20). Then he concentrates upon the prayer of the leader of the nuns, 'O Christ, Christ, come quickly' (*sts.* 24–31), heard above the noise of the wind and breakers; he ponders over the state of her mind and its effect upon the 'comfortless unconfessed' around her. There follows an invocation to God as 'master of the tides' (*st.* 32); Hopkins obviously remembered that though there were on board a master and three pilots, with other officers who were certified 'masters', they had been un-knowingly carried over thirty miles off course by the tides, losing the lives of more than a quarter of those who were entrusted to them. He ends with an invocation to Christ to reclaim England as His own, and to the nun who was drowned in the midst of her witness for the faith, imploring her prayers for his country:

Our King back, Oh, upon English souls! . . .

More brightening her, rare-dear Britain, as his reign rolls,
Pride, rose, prince, hero of us, high-priest, . . .

Rhythm. Hopkins told Dixon that at the time of the wreck 'I had long had haunting my ear the echo of a new rhythm which now I realized on paper'. (See Introduction, pp. 16 ff for Sprung Rhythm.) Hopkins indented the lines to indicate the varying number of stresses: the further to the right they start the fewer the stresses. In each stanza *l*.1 has 2 stresses (but expands to 3 stresses in Part the Second); *ll*.2 and 4 have 3, *ll*.3 and 7 have 4, *ll*.5 and 6 have 5, and the last line of each stanza has 6.

PART THE FIRST

st. 3, *l*.4; *spell*: [in] that crisis or [under] that fell influence. *Cf.* 'hell's spell', No. 54, *l*.13.

l.7; *Carrier-witted*: with the instinct of a dove or pigeon for finding its way home.

l.8; *from the flame to the flame*: probably from the penal flames of hell to the purging flames of Christ's love.

st. 4, *ll*.2–4; *at the wall/Fast . . . fall*: originally 'under the wall fast'. *Cf. st.* 32, *l*.4 where God is called 'the wharf . . . and the wall'. The image is of a boat safely moored at the sea wall, but [under]mined by the current, lifting and sinking with the tide (*cf.* the spiritual security of the believer, who may still be liable to elation and depression).

ll.5–8; *water . . . gift*: like the ship, the water in a well is within the safety of the wall, though it will fall or rise as it is drawn upon or replenished by the streams. These runlets are compared to a rope connecting the well with the high slope of the *voel* (pronounced 'voil' – a Welsh word for a tall hill with no trees).

st. 5, *l*.7; *instressed, stressed*: though God is immanent in nature everywhere, to perceive Him needs a responsive energy in the onlooker (instress), an exertion of mind or will, reacting to the stress or impulse coming from God. *Cf.* 'Hurrahing in Harvest', No. 22, and 'Thee, God, I come from', No. 48, *st.* 2. See also *Sermons*, p. 195: 'All things therefore are charged with love, are charged with God and if we know how to touch them give off sparks and take fire, yield drops and flow, ring and tell of him.'

sts. 6 and 7: the awareness of the divine does not come from His glory in heaven, but from His incarnation and crucifixion.

st. 6, *l*.7; *it rides time*: like a ship anchored in a rushing river, or a lightship secure from the tidal swirl.

st. 8, *ll.*2–6: in a crisis (like a wild sloe crushed by the tongue until it bursts) the real nature of man is revealed, 'sour or sweet'.

*l.*6; *brim, in a flash, full*: brimful in a flash.

*l.*7; *To hero . . . feet*: to the feet of Christ, hero of Calvary; the apostrophe s belongs both to 'hero of Calvary' and to 'Christ', hence the strange second comma.

st. 10, *l.*1; *–ding*: the sound of a blow on heavy metal.

*l.*5; *at a crash Paul*: Saul, a persecutor of Christians, was transformed into Paul the Christian apostle through the dazzling light which blinded him and a voice from heaven (*Acts* 9:1–22).

*l.*6; *Austin*: St Augustine of Hippo, who was brought to Christ, as he tells us, 'little by little with most tender and most merciful hand'.

PART THE SECOND

st. 11: presents Death as a braggart with drum and bugle, boasting of his many instruments of destruction. (But *st.* 32, *ll.*7–8 point to God on His invisible throne behind Death as the real Master.)

*l.*2; *flange and the rail*: railway accidents, then often caused by broken wheel flanges.

*l.*8; *cringe*: because the scythe seems to creep on the ground, like a man cringing.

st. 12, *l.*5; *under thy feathers*: under thy wings, protection (*cf. Psalm* 91:4, 'He shall cover thee with his feathers'; also *Matthew* 23:37).

*ll.*7–8; *dark side of the bay . . . vault*: they were arched over by God's shining providence, though they could see only its dark underside. Hopkins uses bay as an architectural term, as in 'bay window' or the bay in a vaulted roof.

st. 14, *l.*4; *Kentish Knock*: a treacherous sandbank beyond the mouth of the Thames, just over 20 miles SE of Harwich, and roughly the same distance NNE of Margate.

*l.*7; *whorl*: the propeller, which broke when the engines were reversed in a desperate effort to keep the ship off the sandbank.

st. 17, *l.*5; *heart-break*: each bereaved sufferer was the very embodiment of heart-break, but instead of comfort heard only the cries of other heart-broken ones around her.

st. 18: this is addressed by the poet to his own heart, so deeply moved by the shipwreck that it had caused him to end his poetic silence of many years.

*l.*6; *madrigal start*: lyrical burst of sound.

135

st. 19, *l.*3; *hawling*: hauling, dragging sideways.

*l.*4; *rash smart sloggering brine*: violent, sharp, slamming saltwater.

*l.*5; *that weather*: in the storm: 'weather' is used nautically of violent winds and waves; *cf. st.* 25, *l.*6.

*l.*6; *fetch*: probably reach, direction, objective.

*ll.*7–8; *call . . . rode*: *i.e.* her cry to God rose over the sounds of the storm to reach the men in the rigging.

st. 20, *l.*1; *first of a five*: chief sister among the five nuns on board.

*l.*3: the doomed ship had the same name as the country which had driven them out.

*l.*5: St Gertrude was born in Eisleben, later the birthplace of Luther.

*l.*6: she was frequently compared to a lily.

st. 21, *l.*3: Germany exiled them, and they were drowned near the estuary of England's 'national' river, the Thames, a circumstance used here to symbolise Britain's rejection of the Catholic faith.

*l.*5; *Orion*: the constellation was associated in classical times with winter storms, and subsequently in Christian days with the persecution of the martyrs.

*l.*6; *unchancelling*: probably driven out from behind the screen of their convent; *cf.* 'uncloistered', ejected from the cloister.

st. 22, *ll.*1–2; *five*: a sacred number; the doubting disciple Thomas 'found' the resurrected Christ when shown His five wounds, His badge and symbol.

st. 23, *ll.*1–5: St Francis, the founder of the nuns' Order, saw Christ as a fiery seraph on Mt Alverna, and as a proof ('seal') of the visitation he received in his body the pattern of Christ's wounds ('Lovescape crucified').

st. 25, *l.*1; *The majesty*: probably referring to the calm heroism which he saw in the nun.

*l.*2; *arch*: from the Greek noun *archē*, the origin, first cause; *Breath*: here referring to the Spirit of God which existed before creation, and which was breathed into the first man.

*l.*4; *lovely Death*: the crucified Christ.

*ll.*5–6; *men/Woke*: *i.e.* 'who woke'; *We are perishing*: see *Matthew* 8:24–25 for the storm ('weather') on the Sea of Galilee: *cf. st.* 19, *l.*5.

st. 26, *l.*2; *down-dugged*: *cf. Correspondence of G. M. H. and Dixon*, p. 73: 'white precipitate clouds . . . like a herd / Of deep-uddered cows', quoted from Dixon's poem, which Hopkins recognised as an 'Aryan image of the cloud cows'. See N. H. MacKenzie: 'On Editing Gerard

Manley Hopkins', *Queen's Quarterly* 78:4 (Winter 1971), p. 501.

*ll.*7–8: see *I Corinthians* 2:9. 'Eye hath not seen, nor ear heard, neither have entered into the heart of man, the things which God hath prepared for them that love him.' Each man builds up in imagination his own heaven of desire.

st. 27, *ll.*1–5: the poet argues that long drawn-out suffering is more liable than intense danger to provoke a prayer for deliverance through death.

st. 28, *ll.*1–5: the broken syntax images the poet's excitement over the nun's direct appeal for help to Christ, as Master of the seas and storm.

st. 29, *l.*5; *Wording it*: the nun sees Christ as the 'author' of the storm.

*ll.*7–8; *Simon Peter . . . Tarpeian-fast*: see *Matthew* 16:18. 'Thou art Peter, and upon this rock I will build my church; and the gates of hell shall not prevail against it.' The Tarpeian is a rock in Rome, associated in Hopkins's mind with Milton, *Paradise Regained* IV:44–50. 'There the Capitol thou seest / . . . On the Tarpeian rock, her citadel / Impregnable.'

st. 30, *l.*3: the Feast of the Immaculate Conception of the Virgin Mary falls on 8 December, the day after the nun's drowning.

st. 32, *l.*3: part of the lesson for that feast (*st.* 30) used to be *Proverbs* 8:29. 'He enclosed the sea within its confines, forbidding the waters to transgress their assigned limits . . . he poised the foundations of the world' (*Roman Missal* for 8 December).

*l.*5; *ocean of a motionable mind*: the thoughts of men are compared to a restless sea, always threatening to trespass beyond its legitimate limits.

st. 33: God provides an ark for the listener (*i.e.* the obedient), love for the lingerer (the hesitant); a vein (*cf. st.* 4, 'a vein of the Gospel proffer') for those in purgatory or limbo.

*ll.*6–8: see *I Peter* 3:18–20. Christ after death preached to the souls in prison, the furthest boundary ('uttermost mark') which Christ reached ('fetched') in His triumphant journey (compared to another storm).

st. 34, *l.*1; *new born*: as though the uttering of His name by the nun had been a new incarnation (see *st.* 30; *ll.*7–8).

*ll.*6–8: may He return to England like a shower of rain in sunlight, not as an obscure infant (as in Bethlehem), nor as the terrible Judge of the Last Day.

st. 35, *l.*4: may he come back as king over English souls.

10 *'To him who ever thought with love'*

Circa 1876–7. A paraphrase of a passage in *The Life and Revelations of*

St Gertrude, a book from which Hopkins had drawn some touches; *cf.* 'Wreck of the Deutschland', *st.* 20.

11 *Moonrise*

19 June 1876. Written at St Beuno's. Maenefa, a tall hill, rises behind the College. See Introduction, p. 24.

*l.*5: a horn tip, like a barb, still hooked the mountain ('him').

12 *The Woodlark*

5 July 1876. Also written at St Beuno's. The only autograph is a draft with many corrections and some gaps. The version here printed was arranged by Rev. Geoffrey Bliss, S.J., who with great skill supplied words (enclosed in square brackets) to fill the lacunae.

13 *The Silver Jubilee*

Summer 1876. To celebrate the Bishop of Shrewsbury's twenty-fifth year in his episcopate, the members of St Beuno's presented him with an album containing complimentary poems in many different languages. Hopkins's English poem was not only set to music and sung as a glee by the choir, but published along with a commemorative sermon by Fr Morris. Hopkins translated it into both Welsh and Latin.

14 *Penmaen Pool*

1876. The theology students at St Beuno's used to spend a two-week summer vacation at Barmouth, during which it was a tradition to row up the Mawddach estuary to Penmaen Pool, near Dolgelley, Merioneth, and lunch at the George Inn before returning. Hopkins carefully polished this poem to be inscribed in the Visitors' Book there, August 1876. The book has long since vanished. See Introduction, pp. 17, 18.

st. 4: when the water is still, by the laws of reflection, the whole landscape may be seen repeated in the faithful, fairyland mirror of Penmaen Pool.

15 *God's Grandeur*

23 February to March 1877. Written at St Beuno's.

*l.*1: see note to 'Wreck of the Deutschland', *st.* 5.

*l.*2: an earlier version read 'like lightning from shook foil'. Hopkins explained in a letter to Bridges (p. 169): 'Shaken goldfoil gives off broad glares like sheet lightning and also, . . . owing to its zigzag dints and creasings . . . a sort of forked lightning too'.

ll.3–4: the evidence builds up, fragment by fragment, just as the oil from an olive press gathers drop by drop to impressive volume. An earlier version read: 'like an oozing oil / Pressed', clearly with Keats's 'Ode to Autumn' in mind.

ll.4–8: the Victorians were much concerned about the increase in pollution. Hopkins attributed it to an alienation not merely from Nature but from the God behind Nature, Whose 'rod' of authority was ignored.

16 *The Starlight Night*

24 February 1877. Looking up at the myriad stars on a clear frosty winter night, the poet fancies himself looking down from a height on cities and enchanted woods with diamond pits (*ll*.1–5). Some groups of stars look like trees with the silver undersides of their leaves glinting (*l*.6), or an upward swirl of frightened doves (*l*.7), or orchard-trees in spring blossom (*l*.10), or else they gleam yellow just as willows do when covered with pollen in March (*l*.11).

l.13; *shocks*: piles of sheaves.

17 *Spring*

May 1877.

ll.11–13: O Christ, win over the innocent mind of each child in its springtime, before it cloys and clouds with sin.

18 *In the Valley of the Elwy*

23 May 1877. The sonnet opens confusingly, the octave being a grateful memory of kindness received from a family at Shooter's Hill, South London. The Welsh are contrasted with them in the sestet.

19 *The Sea and the Skylark*

May 1877. Written at Rhyl.

ll.5–8: the climbing lark's song, newly wound up, descends, like a fishing line zig-zagging down from a spinning wheel ('winch'). See his detailed interpretation of the first version in *Letters to Bridges*, pp. 163–4.

20 *The Windhover*

30 May 1877. An absorbing poem which has been interpreted in numerous different ways. This reading of it is not intended to be complete or definitive.

l.1; *caught*: grasped, gained insight into the flight and character of the kestrel.

minion: king's favourite and heir ('dauphin').

*ll.*2–5: the bird planes along, steady, the air rolling beneath him; then he sweeps up to an abrupt stop (like a rider reining in a horse), and after hovering for a while with quivering wing in his excitement, he swings down in a banking glide, smooth as a skater on a curve ('bow-bend').

*ll.*9–10: animal beauty ('plume'), valour ('pride') and action ('act' or movement through the air) here combine ('buckle', join in a perfect circle). There has been much controversy over whether 'buckle' is indicative or imperative, whether it means to coalesce or collapse, etc.

*ll.*10–11: beauty shown in courageous action is far more brilliant and effective than passive beauty. (This is only the surface meaning: deeper implications contrast the supreme king, Christ, with His favourite, the falcon, seen as a minor image of the great Chevalier.)

*ll.*12–13: the hard plod of the horse makes the ploughshare shine down the furrow.

*ll.*13–14: the last lines are full of overtones concerning the Crucifixion and Christian self-sacrifice; glory breaks from a seemingly dead ember as it gives out all its last heat in a sacrificial fall.

21 *Pied Beauty*

Summer 1877. A curtal (or shortened) sonnet.

*ll.*7–10: the syntax is: 'He whose beauty is past change [*i.e.* God] fathers forth all things counter [*i.e.* contrary to the norm, unusual]', etc.

22 *The Caged Skylark*

1877. Written at St Beuno's.

*l.*1; *scanted*: cramped.

*ll.*12–14: the resurrection body will provide a home for the spirit without burdening it as our mortal bodies do: a rainbow can rest on downy grass without disturbing it.

23 *Hurrahing in Harvest*

1 September 1877. Written in the Vale of Clwyd (Wales). Hopkins described this poem to Bridges (*Letters*, p. 56) as 'the outcome of half an hour of extreme enthusiasm as I walked home alone one day from fishing in the Elwy'. To his mother he once wrote: 'In its way there can hardly be in the world anything to beat the Vale of Clwyd' (a valley parallel to the Elwy).

l.4; *Meal-drift*: thin specks of cloud, like meal scattered, which appeared and disappeared ('moulded and melted').

ll.9–10: the blue hills combine the strength of a stallion and the sweetness of a violet.

24 *The Lantern out of Doors*

1877. Written at St Beuno's. Probably an autumnal poem which reflects the mists and fogs ('our much-thick and marsh air') rising up from the river valleys in the evenings.

ll.9–11: I lose sight of them through their death or departure; try as I may to follow their progress I cannot go with them to the end.

25 *The Loss of the Eurydice*

April 1878. Written at Mount St Mary's, Derbyshire. Hopkins noted that it was written in sprung rhythm (see Introduction, p. 17), the third line of each stanza having three stresses and the rest four each.

The 'Eurydice' was a naval frigate of 921 tons displacement, which when put into service in the 1840s, being fully-rigged, was one of the fastest in the fleet. She had recently been refitted as a training-ship, and in November 1877 set off with over 300 officers and ordinary seamen from the naval reserves, along with a few boys, on a mid-winter training cruise to the West Indies. Nothing had been heard of her since she had left Bermuda homeward-bound early in March when on Sunday, 24 March 1878, she was sighted by the coastguard at Ventnor, Isle of Wight, pressing towards Portsmouth, resplendent under full sail. She obviously hoped to anchor in Spithead by nightfall. Even the studding sails (mainly used in fair weather) were set, although the glass was falling so rapidly that other ships in the vicinity had shortened sail. Perhaps she was too close to the island cliffs and the steep rise of Boniface Down to have noticed the heavy bank of clouds approaching from the north-west. Her freshly-painted life-buoys hung on ropes over the sides, and her portholes, only six feet above the water line, were open. Suddenly a violent squall, accompanied by a blinding snow-storm, rushed down on her from the cliffs. Captain Hare attempted to take in the sails, but before the royals and top studding sails could be furled or even cut loose, the ship keeled over, filled with water through its open ports, and sank. Of an estimated 368 souls on board, only two survived, an able seaman and Sydney Fletcher, a lad of only nineteen, though already a first-class seaman (see *ll*.57–72). Captain Hare went down with his ship (*ll.*45–56). The disaster was one of the worst in British naval history. Hopkins as a boy had spent many holidays around the places mentioned in his swiftly moving poem (*ll.*29–32). He reported to Bridges on 2 April: 'My muse turned utterly sullen in the Sheffield smoke-ridden air and I had not written a line [since leaving Wales the previous October] till the foundering of the Eurydice the other day and that worked on me and I am making a poem' (*Letters to Bridges*, p. 48). He was concerned as a priest over the abruptness with which death overtook the sailors, allowing no time for repentance.

*ll.*5–6: he thinks of the sailors as a forest of oak trees, felled by a lightning stroke and buried ('furled') in the sand.

*ll.*7–8: the bells of sheep grazing on the steep slopes ('forefalls') of the lofty ('aerial') downs.

*l.*16; *bole and bloom*: seasoned men along with the flower of youth.

*l.*22; *Bright sun*: Hopkins explained the line to Dixon: 'a bright sun was darting fire from the bay of heaven' (*Correspondence*, p. 33).

*l.*25; *beetling baldbright*: the overhanging bold-bright cloud.

*l.*28; *wolfsnow*: cf. 'Wreck of the Deutschland', st. 27, *l.*8, 'endragonèd seas'.

*l.*32; *Boniface Down*: a great domed hill (787 feet) from which the fury of the storm front was apparently channelled down the steep ravine called Luccombe Chine, opposite which the doomed ship was sailing.

*l.*33: at the inquest over the only three dead seamen whose bodies were recovered, and in the newspapers, many questions were asked about the Captain's wisdom in carrying such a press of sail when the barometer was falling and other ships around him were shortening sail.

*l.*40; *messes of mortals*: the messes which were about to come on watch at eight bells were drawing their meal when the squall struck.

*ll.*53–6: a generalisation not aimed at Captain Hare. cf. No. 50 '[The Soldier]'. *l.*11. Hare had been awarded four medals for his naval service.

*l.*68; *rivelling*: (dialect) causing the skin to shrivel. Most of the men who escaped being sucked down when the ship sank were apparently killed by the cold.

*l.*88: he compares England to a sinking vessel.

*l.*99; *riving off*: splitting asunder.

*ll.*101–2: when England was Catholic, travellers at night would call the Milky Way the road to the much-visited shrine at Walsingham, Norfolk, crowded with pilgrims in white.

*l.*112: 'O hero [who] savest'.

ll.113–16: a prayer to Christ. 'And may the prayer I now make prove to have been heard before it was even made, when death struck, and to have been granted in advance on the day when grace was needed [the day of drowning]'.

ll.117–120: redemption is impossible for souls actually in hell, but for those who merely seem to us to be doomed, fresh prayer will fetch pity eternal till the fire of judgement breaks out.

26 *The May Magnificat*

May 1878. Written at Stonyhurst. The idea of regarding May as specially 'Mary's month' seems to have been brought into England about 1840. It was the custom at Stonyhurst and some other Jesuit Colleges to display poems and other pieces in praise of the Blessed Virgin Mary close to her statue during that month. Hopkins's poem in its first form was rejected for this purpose, probably because its unusual sprung rhythm made it appear metrically imperfect to his superiors.

ll.11–12; *opportunest . . . soonest*: most fitting, the first to bring flowers.

l.20; *Throstle*: the current country word for thrush.

ll.20–21; *nested/Cluster of bugle blue eggs*: a nestful of eggs the colour of the bugle or bugloss flower.

l.25; *sizing*: growing in size.

l.40; *silver-surfèd cherry*: cherry trees covered with blossom, like silver surf on the sea.

27 'The furl of fresh-leaved dogrose'

An undated fragment.

28 *Binsey Poplars*

13 March 1879. Written at Oxford. The poplars which were felled had lined the banks of the river Thames, or Isis, as it ran beside the flat Port Meadow, bounding Oxford on the west. The riverside path to Godstow was one of the poet's favourite walks.

29 *Duns Scotus's Oxford*

March 1879. Written at Oxford which had for centuries been a city of beautiful grey stone buildings among trees and gardens where town and country seemed to mingle and blend. But since Hopkins had lived in Balliol as a student, the city had developed an ugly 'skirt' of red-brick terrace houses.

The sestet recreates the Oxford of the early fourteenth century, when Johannes Duns Scotus, his favourite medieval philosopher, lived and lectured there. Scotus was probably the first defender of the doctrine of the Immaculate Conception of the Blessed Virgin Mary.

*l.*12; *realty*: realism in the philosophic sense (a belief in the objective or absolute existence of universals).

30 *Henry Purcell*

April 1879. Written at Oxford. Hopkins sent Bridges (who had been much puzzled by this sonnet) a brief summary of its meaning:

'1–4. I hope Purcell is not damned for being a Protestant, because I love his genius. 5–8. And that not so much for gifts he shares, even though it shd. be in higher measure, with other musicians as for his own individuality. 9–14. So that while he is aiming only at impressing me his hearer with the meaning in hand I am looking out meanwhile for his specific, his individual markings and mottlings, "the sakes of him". It is as when a bird thinking only of soaring spreads its wings: a beholder may happen then to have his attention drawn by the act to the plumage displayed. – In particular, the first lines mean: May Purcell, O may he have died a good death and that soul which I love so much and which breathes or stirs so unmistakeably in his works have parted from the body and passed away, centuries since though I frame the wish, in peace with God! so that the heavy condemnation under which he outwardly or nominally lay for being out of the true Church may in consequence of his good intentions have been reversed. "Low lays him" is merely "lays him low", that is / strikes him heavily, weighs upon him.' (*Letters to Bridges*, pp. 170–1.)

31 *The Candle Indoors*

1879. Written at Oxford. A companion piece to No. 24, 'The Lantern out of Doors'.

*l.*4; *trambeams truckle*: apparently comparing the effect of the flickering candle beams to tiny trams or trucks running backwards and forwards along their rails, between the source of light and the eyeball.

*ll.*12–14: see *Matthew* 5:13. 'You are the salt of the earth. But, if the salt lose its savour, wherewith shall it be salted? It is good for nothing any more but to be cast out and to be trodden on by men.' (*Douay-Rheims*) Also Matthew 7:4. 'How sayest thou to thy brother: Let me cast the mote out of thy eye; and, behold, a beam is in thy own eye?'

32 *The Handsome Heart*

1879. Written at Oxford. Hopkins related the autobiographical details behind the poem:

'The story was that last Lent, when Fr Parkinson was laid up in the country, two boys of our congregation gave me much help in the sacristy in Holy Week. I offered them money for their services, which the elder refused, but being pressed consented to take it laid out in a book. The younger followed suit; then when some days after I asked him what I shd. buy answered as in the sonnet.' (*Letters to Bridges*, p. 86.)

l.5; *carriers*: carrier-pigeons.

33 *The Bugler's First Communion*

July 1879. Written at Oxford. The young hero of this poem, from Cowley Barracks, was shortly afterwards ordered to the Punjab, no doubt because of the war in Afghanistan where the British Resident had been murdered.

ll.42–3: the metaphor from *l*.40 onwards is of a river current, in which floating objects may wind ('rankle') and wander in backward spinning eddies ('backwheels') though eventually carried to their destination by the stream ('though bound home').

l.48: [I may speak] in a presumptuous way ('Forward-like'), but be that as it may ('however'), and very likely ('like'), favourable heaven heard these pleas.

34 *Morning, Midday, and Evening Sacrifice*

August 1879. Written at Oxford.

l.2; *wimpled*: with a Cupid's bow (since wimples curved down on to the centre forehead).

l.6; *fuming*: vapourising away like smoke.

ll.17–21: Hopkins explained to Bridges: 'I meant to compare grey hairs to the flakes of silky ash which may be seen round wood embers burnt in a clear fire and covering a "core of heat" . . . "Your offer, with despatch, of" is said like . . . "Your money or your life" . . .: it is "Come, your offer of all this (the matured mind), and without delay either!"' (*Letters to Bridges*, p. 98.)

35 *Andromeda*

12 August 1879. Written at Oxford. In a sonnet full of resonances, the poet describes the crisis of pain and hope as Andromeda, thonged to the

145

rough rock, hears the loudening roar of the sea monster. Watching the headlands for approaching death, she is unaware of the winged hero above, waiting to destroy her enemy. The sufferings of Andromeda remind us of Christ's, those of the Church, or individual saints waiting to be released from earthly life. Perseus the deliverer is symbolic of St George (if we think of the Catholic Church in England as the sufferer), or of St Michael, but especially of the triumphant Christ.

ll.13–14: Perseus hovers, about to appear when no one expects him, freeing her from bonds and fangs with the Gorgon's gear and his drawn sword ('barebill'). The oblique stroke after 'barebill' indicates a shorter pause than a comma would.

36 *Peace*

1879. Written at Oxford.

ll.1–2: When will you, Peace, wild wood dove, end your roaming round me, and rest under my boughs with your shy wings shut?

l.7; *reaving*: carrying off.

l.9: the original version read 'That will be Peace hereafter'. Patience is the fledgling, Peace the fully-plumed bird.

37 *'As king fishers catch fire'*

Undated [?1878–9]. Each created thing reflects back some particular quality among the infinite aspects of God's unity, and so fulfils its purpose in the universe, just as the open strings of an instrument, and distinctive church bells, sound out the recognisable notes for which they were designed by their human makers. *Cf*. No. 21, 'Pied Beauty'.

l.1: the most characteristic feature of the swift kingfisher is the flash of fiery blue by which it is most often identified.

l.3; *tucked*: (dialect) plucked.

l.4; *bow*: the thickened portion of a bell's rim on which the clapper strikes.

ll.9–14: what the Christian ('the just man') radiates out in the eyes of God is not his own inborn unique character or self, but the beauty of Christ, since Christ's grace is active in him.

l.9; *justices*: acts justly, in a Christlike way.

38 *At the Wedding March*

21 October 1879. Written at Bedford Leigh, Lancashire. Hopkins enjoyed the three months he spent in this grimy town, despite its 'pits and mills and foundries', because his parishioners gave him such a welcome.

39 *Felix Randal*

28 April 1880. Written at Liverpool in memory of a Lancashire black-smith to whom Hopkins had brought comfort in his last illness, confessing him, administering the Mass and anointing him (*ll*.6–8). Touches of Lancashire dialect colour the poem: 'God rest him all road ever he offended' – God give rest to his soul no matter what ways he sinned; and 'fettle', the ordinary countryman's word for make, fix.

40 *Brothers*

August 1880. Written at Hampstead. Hopkins described this as 'a little scene that touched me at Mount St Mary's', a Jesuit College in Chester-field, where he was stationed from October 1877 till April 1878. The poem had taken several years to germinate.

41 *Spring and Fall*

7 September 1880. Written at Lydiate, Lancashire. The poet told Bridges that it was 'not founded on any real incident' (*Letters to Bridges*, p. 109) Margaret, in the young Spring of her life, is crying over the golden leaves dropping from the trees in Autumn. When she is older she will realise that the hidden cause of her tears was her own mortality: then she will weep for the transience of human beauty and strength, not over the shedding of the foliage.

l.8; *wanwood leafmeal*: expressive inventions which suggest the waned beauty of the trees shredded into leafmould.

42 *Inversnaid*

28 September 1881. Named after a hamlet on Loch Lomond and the waterfall close by, over which the impetuous mountain stream called Arklet Water tumbles into the lake. (See also Introduction, p. 16.)

l.3; *In coop and in comb*: in narrows (where the torrent is cooped) and over cascades (where it is combed by a ridge or 'comb' into strands of water).

l.4; *flutes*: is grooved.

l.6; *twindles*: (dialect) splits into twins, possibly also suggesting both dwindle and twist like the dialect 'windle'.

broth | Of a pool: a 'boiling pot' or circular hole in the stream bed from which the vapour of the eddying water rises like steam.

l.9; *degged*: (dialect) sprinkled.

l.11; *heathpacks*: closely knit heath or heather bushes, with low, wiry stems.

flitches: flakes of bracken, stiff and russet-brown, like thin slices from a tree trunk.

l.12; *beadbonny ash*: the rowan or mountain ash, covered with red berries in the autumn.

43 *Ribblesdale*

1882. Written at Stonyhurst, this sonnet was meant as a contrasting companion poem to 'In the Valley of the Elwy' (No. 18), where the landscape seemed perfect. It is a protest against the maltreatment of nature by man, who has inherited forest-covered valleys and pure rivers only to strip and defile them. The creator originally 'dealt down' (divided out) this twisting river bed, and entrusted it to man's care; but the outcome has been 'rack or wrong' (*l*.8). The Ribble flows below Stonyhurst.

l.1; *throng*: (dialect) thick.

l.2; *louchèd*: (dialect) slouching, slovenly – as though contaminated by man.

l.11; *selfbent*: his own selfish inclinations.

turn: purposes.

l.12; *reave*: plunder.

l.13; *none reck of world after*: to care in no way about an after life.

ll.13–14: this is what gives earth so careworn and deeply moving an aspect.

44 *The Leaden Echo and the Golden Echo*

13 October 1882. Written at Stonyhurst, this was intended as an antiphonal song (no doubt the *finale*) in a poetic drama which Hopkins never completed, about the martyrdom of the maiden St Winefred, and the perennial well which miraculously sprang from it. The lines could have been skilfully distributed between segments of the choir, with solo voices assisting, to produce the echo effects alluded to in the title. Hopkins remarked to Dixon: 'I never did anything more musical' (*Correspondence*, p. 149). It is written in sprung rhythm.

THE LEADEN ECHO

l.1; *brace*: clasp.

ll.3–4; *frowning* . . . / *Dówn*: driving away.

THE GOLDEN ECHO

l.1; *Spare*!: Refrain! Deal gently! – As in other echo poems (*e.g.* in Elizabethan times), the second part of a cry (*despair*) is caught up by the echo and transformed into its opposite, here hope for the resurrection body, perpetually young and beautiful (*ll*.11–13).

l.4; *Tall sun*: the sun high in the sky, and strong.

l.10; *wimpled-water-dimpled*: a face dimpled like rippled water.

ll.14–15; *maidengear . . . gaygear . . . girlgrace*: colourful compounds (like those in Anglo-Saxon poetry) such as Hopkins and William Barnes delighted in.

l.18; *beauty-in-the-ghost*: beauty which springs from the spirit. *Cf. Further Letters* (2nd ed., pp. 306–7): 'the bloom of health comes from . . . the vitality within'. Also *cf. Journals*, p. 71: 'On this day by God's grace I resolved to give up all beauty until I had His leave for it'.

ll.22–24; *Nay, what we had lighthanded . . .*: Hopkins paraphrased this for Bridges (21 October 1882): 'Nay more: the seed that we so carelessly and freely flung into the dull furrow, and then forgot it, will have come to ear meantime'. See the Parable of the Sower, *Matthew* 13:3–8.

l.26; *So fagged, so fashed, so cogged*: tired, vexed, grieved. ('cogged' – deceived – is probably a slip for 'cagged', a dialect word which fits better with the context, 'grieved, annoyed, offended'.)

45 *The Blessed Virgin compared to the Air we Breathe*

May 1883. A May-piece, written at Stonyhurst to be displayed in honour of the Virgin Mary near her statue in the College.

l.5; *frailest-flixed*: the most lightly furred.

l.7; *riddles, and is rife*: penetrates and is abundant.

l.16; *minds*: reminds, admonishes (more common in dialect than standard English).

ll.40–1: *i.e.* 'Since God has let her prayers dispense His providence'.

ll.56–8: *i.e.* 'He does now enter into, not flesh, but fresh spirit after fresh spirit, though how He does so is a great mystery'.

ll.66–7: may breathe in more of Christ as if He were breath.

ll.90–3; *soft*: the adjective governing 'Bloom', though separated by a whole line from it.

46 '*The times are nightfall*'

?1884. Written in Dublin, this sonnet was left unfinished, but Hopkins embodied some of its ideas and imagery in the powerful poem which follows it here.

l.8; *dear*: endear.

47 *Spelt from Sibyl's Leaves*

1884–6. Written in Dublin, this weighty and impressive sonnet, in sprung rhythm, has eight feet to each line, divided in the middle by a caesura. Hopkins called it 'the longest sonnet ever made', though he later wrote a still longer one (No. 63). He was concerned that readers should not miss the musical effects he was aiming at (*e.g.* the whole bar or foot of silence indicated by three dots in *l*.1, and the two full-length monosyllabic bars in *l*.2, 'tíme's vást'). He enjoined Bridges: 'Of this long sonnet above all remember what applies to all my verse, that it is, as living art should be, made for performance and that its performance is not reading with the eye but loud, leisurely, poetical (not rhetorical) recitation, with long rests, long dwells on the rhyme and other marked syllables, and so on. This sonnet should be almost sung.' (*Letters to Bridges*, 11 December 1886.)

ll.1–2: evening (captured in the opening crescendo of seven epithets) 'strains' to become time's vast night – the ultimate and universal darkness ('hearse-of-all'), just as it was originally the darkness of chaos from which all things had their birth ('womb-of-all').

l.1: among many others, the adjectives have these overtones: solemn, unconcerned with worldly affairs, impartial, tuning all visible things into unison, vaulted like a burial crypt, enormous, awe-inspiring.

ll.3–4: the construction is: 'Her . . . hornlight . . . [and] her hoarlight . . . waste', *i.e.* the yellow light in the western sky as though from a horn lantern, and the grey light in the zenith, like hoarfrost, both fade.

l.6; *throughther*: (dialect) in confusion.

pashed: (dialect) pulped.

l.7; *disremembering*: bringing oblivion.

round: whisper admonition to.

l.9; *damask*: produce a black wavy pattern, as on damask steel.

l.13; *ware*: (as an adjective) aware, (as a verb) beware!

48 'Thee, God, I come from'

?1885. Written in Dublin. A beautiful hymn, though without an ending. Hopkins thought of adding to it a sort of *credo*, of which we have some fragments.

*l.*11: based on *Hosea* 8:7: 'they have sown the wind, and they shall reap the whirlwind'.

*ll.*17–20: *cf.* No. 46.

49 *To what serves Mortal Beauty?*

23 August 1885. A sonnet with six-foot lines (alexandrines).

*ll.*1–5: asking whether physical beauty, which produces a dangerous pulse in the blood, justifies its existence, the poet answers that it draws us out to the living reality around us. Moreover beauty is goodness made visible, and this can be appreciated at a glance better than through a stare which may embarrass its owner. (See his explanation to Patmore, *Further Letters*, pp. 306–7.)

*l.*2; *the O-seal-that-so feature*: a perfect expression such as we would like to seal (capture on film or in paint, crying to the sitter, 'Hold it!').

flung prouder form: a body carried more nobly than by someone stepping to a Purcell tune (a march or stately dance).

*ll.*6–8: Father Gregory, when handsome young English captives were offered for sale in Rome, picked them out from the crowds by their angel faces (exclaiming '*Non Angli, sed Angeli*' – not Angles but angels). Their beauty thus led to their nation being given the opportunity of listening to Augustine whom St Gregory sent as a missionary to Britain.

*ll.*12–13: with undisturbed heart, acknowledge ('own') the beauty as heaven's sweet gift.

*l.*14: Yes, wish its owner, and indeed everyone, grace, which is a higher form of beauty.

50 *[The Soldier]*

August 1885. Written at Clongowes. The sonnet should include in its title the sailor, since both navy and army are used as symbols of the Christian forces in their fight under Christ the King. That this poem was written in a year of defeat (the fall of Khartoum and the retreat of the British from the Sudan), and in Ireland, where the redcoats were resented, prevents his analogy with the Christian battle from sounding jingoistic. The emphasis is upon courage, not conquest. *cf.* No. 64. Jesuits sometimes spoke of themselves as 'enlisting' in the Society of Jesus (*e.g.* Hopkins in *Sermons*, p. 261), following the military metaphor used by their founder, St Ignatius.

*l.*6; *dears*: endears, values the professional in accordance with his profession.

l.7: and would like to think all that glitters (in the military uniform) is pure gold ('sterling').

51 *'What shall I do for the land'*

Begun at Clongowes in August 1885 and completed in September 1888. Feeling that there was a great need for a patriotic song for soldiers with words worth singing, Hopkins produced this one, together with 'a tune, very flowing and spirited'. He hoped Bridges would approve, for (he added) 'it is worth doing and yet it is a task of great delicacy and hazard to write a patriotic song that shall breathe true feeling without spoon or brag. How I hate both! and yet feel myself half blundering or sinking into them in several of my pieces, a thought that makes me not greatly regret their likelihood of perishing.' (*Letters to Bridges*, p. 283.)

52 *[Carrion Comfort]*

Circa 1885. This sonnet relates two desperate struggles which can be only approximately expressed in a brief paraphrase. The first fight (*ll*.1–4) is against despair, the temptation to lapse into death or a breakdown close to death through sheer exhaustion. Barely victorious, the speaker then finds himself (*ll*.5–8) attacked by a terrifying force, ruthless as a lion, strong as a hurricane, without pity for his wounds or fears. Yet the destruction does not fall. Instead, his slack sinews are wrestled into new strength, his will becomes purer and joy replaces despair (*ll*.9–11). The nightmare darkness over at last, he recognises with ashamed astonishment and relief that his mortal enemy was in fact Christ the divine hero, mastering his soul (*ll*.12–14).

53–57 *[Sonnets of Desolation]*

The five graphic sonnets which follow are often referred to as 'The Sonnets of Desolation'. The title derives from *The Spiritual Exercises* of St Ignatius Loyola, who describes the way in which those striving after spiritual ideals may find themselves in desolation – in darkness and confusion of soul, without hope or love, and seemingly cut off from the Creator.

Writing to Bridges on 1 September 1885, Hopkins said 'I shall shortly have some sonnets to send you, five or more. Four of these came like inspirations unbidden and against my will. And in the life I lead now, which is one of a continually jaded and harassed mind, if in any leisure I try to do anything I make no way – nor with my work, alas! but so it must be.' The sonnets were never sent, but after his death were found among his papers.

53 'No worst, there is none'

Circa 1885.

*l.*1; *No worst*: there is no limit to possible misfortune or pain.

*ll.*1–2; *pitched past pitch . . . wilder wring*: even when the extremity of sorrow seems to have been reached, more torments – made worse by earlier sufferings – will bring greater pain.

*l.*8; *fell*: ruthless.

force: perforce.

*ll.*10–11; *Hold . . . there*: [those] who have never hung there may make light of the experience.

*l.*13; *a comfort serves*: a comfort [which] serves.

54 'To seem the stranger'

Circa 1885. This sonnet speaks of the three removes (*ll.*9–10) which had contributed to the situation in which Hopkins seemed a stranger to those around him. His conversion to the Roman Catholic faith had made his family, who were Anglicans, feel that he was lost to them (*ll.*2–4). Secondly, apart from Bridges and Dixon, such English critics as had seen his work had not recommended it for publication, so that he had lost inspiration and ceased to make any efforts to become known to the public (*ll.*5–8, 11–14). Finally, he was stationed in Ireland, where hostility to England and Englishmen was common – though he had many Irish friends (*ll.*9–11).

*ll.*7–8; *I weary . . . rife*: I weary of being just an idle bystander where conflicts [between Irish and English] are prevalent.

*ll.*11–12; *word/Wisest*: wisest word.

*l.*14; *a lonely began*: like someone left on his own at the starting point.

55 'I wake and feel the fell of dark'

Circa 1885.

*l.*1; *fell*: four or five homophones, each of different origin and meaning, contribute to the total impression: 1, gall or bitterness (*cf. l.*9); 2, a savage blow (a sense contributed to by 3, the adjective 'fell', cruel); 4, a hide, skin or fleece (like an oppressive pall above him); 5, a waste hillside (over whose dark ways he has wandered). See this word discussed at length in MacKenzie: *Hopkins* (Oliver and Boyd, 1968), pp. 89–90.

*ll.*9–10: God would have me taste His most bitter deep decree.

*l.*11: *Bones built* the curse *in me, flesh filled* it, *blood brimmed* it over.

*l.*12; *selfyeast*: zest has to be infused from outside ourselves, like yeast added to dough, or we go sour.

*l.*14; *but worse*: rather ambiguous in its effect. Intellectually he acknowledges that the damned are worse off than he is.

56 'Patience, hard thing'

Circa 1885.

*ll.*1–4: the man who prays for patience to endure his sufferings, rather than for their removal, could be held to be asking for troubles, weariness and defeat.

*l.*8; *purple eyes*: the climbing ivy, often used to cover over unsightly old walls or ruins, has blue-black berries. Its yellowish flowers yield abundant nectar: hence the allusion in *ll.*13–14 to Patience filling honeycombs.

57 'My own heart'

Circa 1885.

*l.*6; *my comfortless*: the adjective seems more telling on its own than the abstract noun 'comfortlessness' would have been. It parallels 'their dark' (*l.*7) and 'world of wet' (*l.*8).

*l.*9; *Jackself*: the drudging part of Hopkins – derived from the use of the name Jack to denote a common labourer.

*ll.*11–12; *size . . . to God knows what*: grow at God's chosen moments and as great as He ordains it.

*ll.*13–14; *unforeseen . . . mile*: his smile comes, rather, at unexpected times and, like vari-coloured skies shining between mountains, makes a mile of the road lovely. To 'pie' is to dapple.

58 [Ashboughs]

Circa 1885.

A curtal (or shortened) sonnet, like 'Pied Beauty' and 'Peace'. In sprung rhythm.

*l.*5; *clammyish lashtender combs*: the first moist sprays on the tree-tops, tender as lashes.

*ll.*8–10; *May . . . greenery*: the May sky, seen through the branches, then only just beginning to come into leaf, shows a mingling of blue heavens and snowy clouds.

ll.10–11: just as the tree needs the earth and the sun, so we are the product of a marriage between earth and heaven, the material and the divine.

59 *On the Portrait of Two Beautiful Young People*

Christmas 1886. Written at Monasterevan, this poem, unfortunately never finished, sprang from the sight of an old painting showing a brother and sister, young and full of promise. The poet's admiration is tinged with sadness by the knowledge that beauty brings its special temptations (*ll*.29–32), and that as the young develop into maturity they may fail to realise that even the best need a strength greater than their own. He projects himself back in time to view them as the artist saw his sitters, conjecturing their future. See also Introduction, p. 14.

l.4; *vein*: mood; with this line *cf*. 'The Leaden Echo' (No. 44).

ll.6–7; *blest/In one fair fall*: by the birth of two fine children at once. (Hopkins seems to imply that they were twins, departing for the purposes of his poem from the literal facts given him.)

l.8; *heft*: strain.

ll.9–12: preserved in the portrait, the caressing beams still illumine the golden hour of their youth, which would otherwise have vanished like a dream or foam on the swirling Barrow. (The river ran beside Monasterevan.)

l.20; *stead*: serve, help.

l.24: the rich young ruler who was 'good', but not good enough (*Mark* 10:17–22).

l.25; *list*: inclination (*i.e.* as he grows up, a man displays the innate leanings which were hidden when he was young).

l.28; *foredrawn to*: biased towards.

l.29: earlier drafts show that the poet thought of the lad's feast of good looks as being summed up in his earnest gaze; the two parts of the line are in apposition.

l.31; *worst will the best*: originally 'worst will batten on best'.

60 *Harry Ploughman*

September 1887. Written at Dromore. Hopkins here aimed at a 'direct picture of a ploughman, without afterthought'. In a later letter to Bridges, he added: 'I want Harry Ploughman to be a vivid figure before the mind's eye'. He intended the poem for recital, and suggested that the shorter (or burden-) lines might be given to a chorus, so as to produce a sort of echo. (See *Letters to Bridges*, pp. 262, 263, 265.)

In the first part of the sonnet (*ll*.1–11), the artist draws in detail the finely trained crew of members and muscles which constitute the ploughman's physical equipment for his strenuous task. Then (*l*.12) Harry leans his weight on the handles, and his horses strain into action. The plough wallows like a ship in a rough sea, but Harry's graceful liquid strength is in control. His fair hair lifts in the cross breeze and tosses, while his feet keep pace with the iron share and the cascading slices of earth.

l.1; *broth of goldish flue*: haze of golden down.

l.3; *rope-over thigh*: because the muscles seem like plaited rope.

knee-nave: knee-cap.

l.7; *curded*: curdled, knotted.

l.13; *quail*: yield, tremble.

l.15; *wind-lilylocks-laced*: *i.e.* his lilylocks interlaced by the wind.

l.17; *frowning*: wrinkled (*i.e.* his creased hide boots).

61 *Tom's Garland*

September 1887. Written at Dromore. The first draft of this sonnet was comparatively easy to read, but in the course of developing its verbal music and adding two codas (*ll*.15–17 and 18–20), Hopkins made it so complicated that neither Bridges nor Dixon could decipher it. Though amused at their defeat, Hopkins agreed 'It is plain I must go no farther on this road: if you and he cannot understand me who will?' The author then provided them with a long explanation (*Letters to Bridges*, pp. 272–4), the beginning and end of which are quoted below, the middle portion being used to guide the section-by-section paraphrase in between.

Basic imagery: 'as St Paul and Plato and Hobbes and everybody says, the commonwealth or well ordered human society is like one man; a body with many members and each its function; some higher, some lower, but all honourable, from the honour which belongs to the whole. The head is the sovereign, who has no superior but God and from heaven receives his or her authority: we must then imagine this head as bare (see St Paul much on this) and covered, so to say, only with the sun and stars, of which the crown is a symbol, which is an ornament but not a covering; it has an enormous hat or skull cap, the vault of heaven. The foot is the daylabourer, and this is armed with hobnail boots, because it has to wear and be worn by the ground; which again is symbolical; for it is navvies or daylabourers who, on the great scale or in gangs and millions, mainly trench, tunnel, blast, and in other ways disfigure, "mammock" the earth and, on a small scale, singly, and superficially stamp it with their footprints.'

*ll.*1–3: the day's work done, Tom, a garland of hobnails under foot, piles his pick, followed by his mate, sturdy Dick (who wears like loamy-coloured boots), and each strikes sparks from the stones on his homeward path.

*ll.*4–5: Tom the navvy is now intent on his meal, of course, and his bed. Though his lot is a humble one, that thought does not weigh him down.

(*l.*8 supplies the missing verb: 'He *swings* his low lot lustily though.')

*ll.*6–8: [In parenthesis] (Tom that never needs to go hungry, who is seldom sick, less often heartsore; who is as untroubled by sharp mental perplexities as his boots are by thorns.)

*ll.*8–12: I little care whether all are equal in our human society provided all are fed. To serve our country is honour enough for us all – for the sovereign head, lit by the sun and stars of heaven, or the mighty foot, that trenches into mother earth.

*ll.*12–14: but if neither mind nor physical strength are called into service [as with the unemployed], no benefits are given their possessors – neither the golden crown and hazards [of the country's rulers], nor the freedom from care in the labourer's routine.

*ll.*15–18: they have been made outcasts, denied both glory and ease of mind; they have no place allotted them and so are given no garland, neither honour nor protection; but as for care! *That* we permit them to share!

*ll.*18–20: Care and Despair mated to breed the dull Hangdog; Care and Rage bred the worse Manwolf; and their packs infest the age.

The intended tone of lines 13 to the end emerges more clearly in Hopkins's paraphrase: 'this is all very well for those who are in, however low in, the Commonwealth and share in any way the Common weal; but . . . the curse of our times is that many do not share it, that they are outcasts from it and have neither security nor splendour; that they share care with the high and obscurity with the low, but wealth or comfort with neither. And this state of things, I say, is the origin of Loafers, Tramps, Cornerboys, Roughs, Socialists and other pests of society.'

This letter should be compared with an earlier one to Bridges powerfully presenting the grievances of the 'greatest and most necessary part of a very rich nation', who are themselves largely responsible for the nation's wealth, but who are compelled 'to live a hard life without dignity, knowledge, comforts, delight, or hopes in the midst of plenty'. (*Letters to Bridges*, pp. 27–28.)

62 *Epithalamion*

1888. Written in Dublin. 'I began an Epithalamion on my brother's wedding: it had some bright lines, but I could not get it done.' So Hopkins lamented in a letter to Bridges in May 1888, the month after Everard had been married. The allegory seems to have proved unworkable.

l.4; *dean . . . clough . . . cleave*: local words for a narrow wooded valley, usually with a stream running through it ('dean', much used around Hampshire, becomes 'dene' in Northern England).

l.9; *honeysuck*: honeysuckle. Hopkins used the older form, which had survived for 1200 years in country speech.

l.10; *dither*: tremble.

l.17; *bellbright*: bronzed and glistening.

huddling out: diving in excited confusion, close together.

l.24; *hornbeam fretty overstood by*: overshadowed by the hornbeam with its saw-toothed leaves.

l.28; *dings*: flings.

ll.36–37; *coffer, burly . . . rocks*: (rock) pools built of massive natural blocks, their angles hewn by nature, and their surfaces grey.

l.38; *quicksilvery shivès*: runlets like shivers of mercury.

63 *That Nature is a Heraclitean Fire*

July 1888. Written in Dublin. The Greek philosopher Heraclitus, who flourished about 500 B.C., believed that all matter was in a state of flux, the basic elements constantly interchanging themselves. Fire transformed itself first into water and then into earth, and finally back again into fire. Hopkins, adding the traditional fourth element, air, illustrates the theory by describing nature at work on a sunny day after a storm. The sun is parching the oozing mud into its ingredients, earth and water. Overhead the roistering clouds, full of the liquor evaporated from the rain-soaked land, hurry on their drunken way to another scene where air and water will separate in a downpour, and the perpetual cycle will roll on. But (*l*.10) when a man's spark is quenched, he seems to be swallowed by eternal darkness. The sonnet's codas (*ll*.16–24), however, reverse the mood of gloom by reminding us of the Resurrection of the Dead, when the immortal part of man will be seen triumphantly to be like indestructible diamond.

*ll.*3–4: splinters of light and a cordage of shadows interlace, pierce each other and pair off in long lashes, down roughcast or bright whitewashed walls, wherever an elm tree arches above them. See Intro. p. 14.

*l.*5; *ropes*: see this discussed in MacKenzie, *Hopkins*, p. 123.

*ll.*5–9: the boisterous bright wind [combining fire with air] ropes, wrestles, beats . . . parches . . . stanches, starches . . . (All these verbs show the wind's activity.)

*ll.*6–7: the wind dries out the runny mud in pools and cart-tracks, first into 'squeezed dough', then crust-cakes and finally into dust.

*ll.*8–9; *squadroned masks . . . footfretted in it*: [obliterates] the legion of disfiguring footprints trodden into the loam by trudging labourers.

*l.*10; *clearest-selvèd*: most distinctly individual.

*l.*14; *sheer off, disseveral, a star*: sharply separate, like a star.

*ll.*19–20: [let] flesh fade and the worthless carcase be inherited by worms; [let] the world end in a fire which reduces all to ashes.

*ll.*21–24: at the last trumpet I shall suddenly be in a resurrected body because Christ was once in a human body like mine, and this laughable mixture of mortal rubbish with immortal soul will become immortal soul!

64 *St Alphonsus Rodriguez*

October 1888. This poem was written in Dublin at the request of his superiors, and sent to Majorca to honour the first feast day of St Alphonsus Rodriguez after his canonization. St Alphonsus (who died in 1617) for nearly the last forty years of his life was hall porter to the Jesuit College at Palma, Majorca. Hopkins added in a letter to Bridges (3 October 1888), 'he was, it is believed, much favoured by God with heavenly lights and much persecuted by evil spirits'.

*l.*1; *so we say*: 'I mean "This is what we commonly say, but we are wrong".' (*Letters to Bridges*, p. 297.)

*ll.*6–7: but if the warfare is within, [if] the sword we wield is invisible and we wear no steel breast-plate which can be seen.

*l.*9: refers to the gradual shaping of the mountains over the ages through erosion etc.

*l.*10; *trickling increment*: (the opposite process in living things) imperceptible additions.

65 'Thou art indeed just, Lord'

17 March 1889. The Latin epigraph is from the Vulgate version of *Jeremiah* 12:1: 'Thou indeed, O Lord, art just, if I plead with thee, but yet I will speak what is just to thee: Why doth the way of the wicked prosper?' (*Douay-Rheims*); or, as Ronald Knox translates it: 'Lord, I know well that right is on thy side, if I plead against thee, yet remonstrate with thee I must; why is it that the affairs of the wicked prosper . . .?'

*l.*11; *fretty chervil*: wild chervil or cow parsley, with deeply serrated leaves and broad umbrella-like heads of white flowers, among the early spring displays on banks and in hedges.

*l.*13; *time's eunuch*: a year earlier Hopkins had lamented to Bridges: 'Unhappily I cannot produce anything at all, not only the luxuries like poetry, but the duties almost of my position, its natural outcome . . . Nothing comes: I am a eunuch – but it is for the kingdom of heaven's sake' (*Letters to Bridges*, p. 270). Hopkins was quoting from *Matthew* 19:12.

66 'The shepherd's brow'

3 April 1889. This striking and unusual sonnet sets puny man, with his grand airs and his storms in a teacup, in perspective against the stupendous powers of nature. Man makes an unimpressive tragic hero, vulnerable as he is from crawling infancy to bent old age.

*ll.*6–7: *cf.* Shakespeare's 'Seven Ages of Man' (*As You Like It*, II:vii). *memento mori*: every breath is a reminder of death.

*l.*8: what deep tragic notes can we sound out on our little treble viol?

*l.*13: the three dots indicate, not a gap, but a pause during which the poet breaks off his rodomontade, to end the sonnet in personal self-depreciation.

67 To R.B.

22 April 1889. Written in Dublin, Hopkins's last poem was addressed to his life-long friend, Robert Bridges. He had scarcely finished it before he contracted typhoid fever, from which he died on 8 June. His sonnet deals with the nature of poetic inspiration, regretting how seldom it has visited him in recent years.

*l.*6: the poet has to nourish and shape the embryonic idea until its long gestation is completed and the poem is born.

Index of titles and first lines

161

Set in 11 point Bulmer type leaded 2 points

Printed by W & J Mackay Limited, Chatham

on Abbey Mills Antique Laid paper.

Bound by W & J Mackay Limited

in quarter leather with cloth sides

Елена Чижова